The River Cottage
Veg Patch Handbook

The River Cottage
Veg Patch Handbook

by Mark Diacono

introduced by
Hugh Fearnley-Whittingstall

www.rivercottage.net

BLOOMSBURY
LONDON · BERLIN · NEW YORK

for Candida

First published in Great Britain 2009

Text © 2009 by Mark Diacono

Photography © 2009 by Mark Diacono

Additional photography on pp.51, 197 (left), 205, 224, 231, 232,
235, 236, 241, 245, 249, 252 © 2009 by Gavin Kingcome

The moral right of the author has been asserted

Bloomsbury Publishing Plc, 36 Soho Square, London W1D 3QY

A CIP catalogue record for this book is available from the British Library

ISBN 978 0 7475 9534 2

10 9 8 7 6 5 4 3

Project editor: Janet Illsley

Design: willwebb.co.uk

Printed and bound in Italy by Graphicom

Mixed Sources
Product group from well-managed
forests, controlled sources and
recycled wood or fibre
www.fsc.org   Cert no. CQ-COC-000015
FSC   © 1996 Forest Stewardship Council

www.bloomsbury.com/river cottage

Contents

I wish I'd had this book in my hands when I first set out on my River Cottage adventure more than ten years ago. I can say with some certainty that it would have saved me from many mistakes, but its author would no doubt find that unduly negative. And this is the joy of Mark's thoroughly upbeat approach to growing your own food. His philosophy is that 'There are no mistakes, just experiences you probably shouldn't repeat.' I can safely say that, if I'd had this book ten years ago, I would not only have had fewer experiences that I don't wish to repeat, I would also have had many more experiences that it would be an unqualified pleasure to repeat again and again, season after season.

I have watched Mark's progress from enthusiastic amateur to passionate teacher with admiration and great pleasure. I'm thrilled that he's now our head gardener at River Cottage. Both on our courses and in the pages of this book, I can think of no better person to share our philosophy with a wider audience. There are few people better placed than Mark to tell you how to deploy home-grown veg to improve the quality of your life, because that's precisely what he's been doing for the best part of the last decade. His great strength lies in choosing and growing vegetables and fruits that are 100 per cent relevant and therefore 100 per cent rewarding. In other words, he grows food that he knows he will use, and will bring him and his family great enjoyment. He recognises of course that these guiding principles will result in a different harvest for everyone. But one of the joys of this book is the way it helps you decide what that harvest should be for you.

One of Mark's personal passions is to explore the fringes of what it's possible to grow in our unpredictable but undeniably shifting climate. With characteristic verve, he seized the opportunity to look at gardening in a fresh way and started planting pecans, olives and apricots at Otter Farm, his own smallholding in Devon. The inevitably mixed results have included some fantastic successes – among them the most delicious apricots I have tasted anywhere in the world!

Mercifully, Mark's a better grower than a fisherman. When we first met, we went fishing together out of Weymouth, in pursuit of bass. Sadly, Mark spent most of the time with his head over the side of the boat, generously redistributing his breakfast to the local marine life. He didn't say much that morning. Yet when we got talking back on dry land, I quickly realised this was someone who had something interesting to say about food. Then he began running a few courses for us at River Cottage and I saw what a great teacher he is. It's down to him that we now have Szechuan pepper, allspice, almonds and olives nestling on the slopes around River Cottage. But also that we have sent many hundreds of visitors home with the inspired notion that they will, from that moment on, make home-grown food a vital part of their family life.

In addition to his experimental high-risk crops, Mark's 'let's not take anything for granted' approach has led him – and us – to push at the margins of our seasonality and try out innovative growing methods with some of our best-loved veg crops. Consequently you'll find this book is far more than just a digestion of received veg garden wisdom. It is a passionate polemic for growing your own that is full of fresh insights and surprising practical suggestions, such as growing your spuds in stacks of car tyres.

I don't think it's overstating it to say that growing your own food will change your life. It may start with a few pots of herbs, a row of radishes, a tub of lettuce, but it rarely ends there. Change is incremental, but inevitable. The pure, sweet pleasure of podding your own peas seconds after picking them will lead to new adventures, new crops. If you grow it, you're more likely to eat it, to share it with friends, and even find yourself making new friends (that happens a lot when people come to River Cottage HQ).

Once you have made the connection between plot and plate, you'll expect more, and demand more, from your food. Anaemic, shrink-wrapped cabbage from the supermarket can never taste as good as one you tended from a seed, saved from slugs and caterpillars, nurtured through too little rain or too much. You'll cherish it for the miracle it is and, because of that, you're less likely to waste it.

Food miles, packaging and food waste are three of the biggest challenges that face us as a society, but when you grow your own, you are no longer contributing to the problem. And, without doubt, when you're connected to the land you have more of a stake in its welfare.

Mark and I believe that this adventure is out there for everyone. You just have to choose it. Whether you live in the middle of the city or are nestled in your own green acres, whether you have a terrace with tubs, a regimental allotment or a sprawling vegetable garden, you can have a go. Growing vegetables is a forgiving activity. Try new things, experiment, and as long as you hang on to your optimism and sense of wonder, your veg patch – however tidy or raggedy, big or small – will be a kingdom of earthy delights. As Mark says, 'Plants want to grow, all we have to do is let them, rather than make them'.

I'm very excited about this book. Whether you want to grow a few beans or tend a huge spread, Mark's your man. His wisdom will stand you in great stead as you embark on the adventure of growing your own. And at a time when it's easy to fall prey to all of the gloom that surrounds the food we eat, Mark's sense of what is possible is the perfect antidote.

Hugh Fearnley-Whittingstall, East Devon, March 2009

Growing your
own Food

There are few pleasures that beat sitting in your veg patch in May with people you love, your just-cut asparagus cooking on a camping stove and almost ready to eat with a little butter, salt, pepper and Parmesan. Pour a glass of something dry made from grapes or apples and you'll be enjoying the best that the good life has to offer.

Such moments – and there are many of them – are unique to the home-grower. As the asparagus ends, so come the peas, the beans, the baby carrots – each one incomparable to its shop-bought cousin. And so it goes through each of the seasons. If you're looking for a reason to start a veg patch, these moments alone make a compelling case.

You may also find (as I did) that you become a better cook. When you have played a part in its growth, you understand why this tomato tastes so special or why that one's only okay, and why waiting to pick your parsnips until after the frosts makes them taste so sweet. But you'll get much more than amazing food from your plot.

One of the essential beauties of having a veg patch is that the simple act of growing and eating your own food decorates life in often unexpected ways. Whether you need more time alone or more time with loved ones, space to think or more time doing, your plot can provide. If you have children, take some time to involve them; if they see sweetcorn pop up in a pot, having sown it a few days earlier, they're almost certain to follow it along its journey until they are eating their own popcorn. And once you start, it sows the seeds for more.

You may well find that your veg patch turns food into something you do rather than just what you eat. It takes you into the outside world and brings it into your home; it roots you in your landscape, and acts as the seasonal clock around which family, friends – and the soil that supports them – come together. Simply, I know of no one with a veg patch whose life hasn't been greatly enhanced as a result.

Aside from the personal, there has never been a more important time to grow your own food. Our dependence on oil-based chemicals to beef up the plant and beat up its competition means that it typically takes ten times more energy to grow it than it delivers as food. Add to that the packaging, the food miles and the energy budgets of supermarkets (using more per square metre than most factories), and it's hardly surprising that our shopping basket accounts for as much as a quarter of our carbon footprint.

With our climate changing and oil peaking, we have little choice but to move towards a low-carbon diet and there's simply no better way of doing that than by growing our own organic food. As writer Michael Pollan put it: 'Growing even a little of your own food is one of those solutions (to climate change) that, instead of begetting a new set of problems – the way "solutions" such as ethanol or nuclear power inevitably do – actually beget other solutions, and not only of the kind that save carbon.' It creates new habits that give us low-carbon food at its best and that dilute our reliance on big business and reconnect with our ability (and need) to provide for ourselves. It strikes a blow for independence.

If it sounds laughably idealistic to contend that a veg patch can really make a difference, remember that our dependencies on oil and supermarkets for our food are only as they are thanks to so many similarly small, repeated actions: we vote them in every time we shop, and we vote them out every time we sow.

A veg patch is also the perfect place to remind ourselves of one of the fundamentals of life itself: we depend on plants. For all our evolutionary advances, they can do something we can't: create food for themselves from little more than sunlight and air. Happily, many of them do it in such a way that's not only edible for us, it's delicious. And we get much more than flavour from eating seasonal food that is harvested at the top of its game and full of vitality. Vitamins, minerals and antioxidants are all at their peak when first picked, so every mouthful brings with it more of what your body needs. It also gives them to us as we need them – in frequent, small, combined doses. So it's not just that we need to eat plants, we were built to eat them.

This book is about everything to do with that fundamental relationship. It's still a food book, it just happens to be about the whole journey – from plot to plate. Most of us are a little more familiar with the eating than the growing, but start your own veg patch and I hope you'll quickly find the plants a fascinating means to a delicious end.

You needn't feel intimidated if you are new to growing. It isn't the great mystery that so many would have it. On the contrary, it's compellingly, wonderfully simple. It is even (dare I say it) fairly hard to mess up; you just may not know how to do some of it yet. Think of it like directions to a new place – follow them and getting there is simple, and you'll soon be doing it without thinking. Growing is mostly a matter of helping everything along – caring for the soil, bringing things together at the right time and removing any obvious obstacles. Plants want to grow, all we have to do is *let* them rather than make them.

Nor do you need an acre, an allotment or even a garden: a veg patch is simply a space, however small, where you can grow even a little of what you eat. Everyone can do it and this book offers you a series of invitations to do just that.

So if it's time, space, money or inspiration you're short of, don't worry: all are common obstacles but none of them are insurmountable, as I hope this book will reassure you. Clear a patch or fill a few pots with compost and you'll be glad you did. Your food will not only be the finest you've ever tasted, it will come with no packaging, no branding, no food miles, no hydrogenated this or saturated that. Food simply doesn't get any better, but more than that, you'll find everything about it is positive – for you, your family and even for the wider world.

Making a wish list

When I began growing food I spent so much time pondering which plants fitted in where that I almost forgot the point – getting mouthwatering food to the table. A lazy bath reading *Jane Grigson's Vegetable Book* jolted my mind back on track in a second. I got out all the food books and put away the growing ones and started scribbling an unfettered list of food I liked. Everything went in regardless of whether it would grow in the UK, avocado included, and I'd recommend you do the same. Think firstly of flavour and you won't go far wrong.

The Vegetable A–Z (pp.20–153) is a great place to start with your wish list. I hope it will remind you of some of your favourite flavours as well as challenge you to step out of the familiar – to try new tastes, new varieties and run the risk that you might find a few prejudices threatened.

From that initial wish list you can start whittling or embellishing, depending on the limitations and opportunities of your life and your veg patch. There is no ready-made plan for the ideal patch – all the best gardens (edible or otherwise) express the grower's personality, fit their life, their tastes, and reflect their inquisitiveness, so try to make sure yours does too. What you grow really is up to you, but deciding can be daunting. Here are a few pointers that may help:

Grow what you most like to eat

Although it can (and should) be much more, a successful vegetable patch has to be functional, providing you with at least some of the food you most enjoy. If your plot

is delivering in spades it will justify the time spent out there with your hands in the soil. It may seem obvious, but you'd be surprised how many people grow what they think they should be growing rather than the food they most like to eat.

Challenge your taste buds

Always, always, always grow something you've never eaten before. No matter how long you've been growing your own, no matter how gargantuan your appetite, there will always be something you've yet to munch on. Supermarkets tend to offer the same food week in week out – it simplifies the supply chain and maximises profits. Over time this establishes and reinforces a peculiar mistrust of the unfamiliar: just how good can borlotti beans be if I have never seen them before? The answer: wonderfully, reassuringly appetising. If you're new to them, try Jerusalem artichokes, salsify, kai lan and mizuna, and you'll see what I mean.

You might also consider planting at least one vegetable that you actively dislike, or think you dislike. The likelihood is you'll offer at least a begrudging acceptance that your hated veg is in fact not bad at all. This is partly because the bond between grower and growee confers upon you the pride of the parent, but largely because you'll have the harvest as it should be – at its perfect peak, which is often alarmingly dissimilar to its shop-bought brother. Broadcaster John Peel once said of The Fall that if they were to bring out an album that he didn't like he'd feel it was somehow a failing in him. I'd urge you to think that way a little about food, and assume that you just haven't found the way that it's delicious yet. If, even in its just-picked prime, you find you still can't abide it then you can at least consign it to Room 101 safe in the knowledge you gave it (and yourself) a fair go.

Go for variety

A little of lots rather than lots of a little is what you're after from your veg patch. Sow a broad range of veg and you'll open up all sorts of kitchen possibilities. You'll also find that there can be a huge difference between varieties of the same food – 'Edzell Blue' and 'Pink Fir Apple' potatoes, for instance, not only look, cook and taste completely different, they are harvested months apart. More importantly, by growing a few varieties you'll be taking out a little edible insurance – some varieties resist diseases more readily than others, and having a range greatly reduces your chances of being cleaned out.

Grow through the seasons

Many of the harvests in the colder months will be up there with anything the summer can throw at you – the purple sprouting broccoli, salsify and giant red mustard leaves in winter are a match for the best any season can offer, so I would encourage you to plan and plant for the whole year.

Some gardeners treat their patch a little like their tent – happy to enjoy it in the sunnier months and even happier to pack it away as the nights draw in. There is absolutely nothing wrong with taking this approach if it suits you best, but do it consciously. Many's the allotmenter who tidies away the last bedraggled courgette and squash plants wondering what's coming next, to find themselves with nothing to follow. Rest assured you can have year-round home-grown feasts, but you have to plan for them in the same way you do for the stars of the main summer show.

Prioritise plot-to-plate veg

Some harvests keep hold of their best characteristics for weeks or even months – parsnips, for example – and we should love them for it. Others, such as asparagus, sweetcorn and peas, are altogether more delicate, happy to lose texture, vigour or (most distressingly) their sugars from the second they are detached from the plant. Without exception, they're delicious, so do grow some and get them from plot to pot as soon as you can – hours are crucial, even minutes for some – and you'll have the best that any veg patch can offer.

Top 8 plot-to-plate veg

Asparagus	see p.28
Peas (and pea shoots)	see p.110
Broad beans	see p.39
New potatoes	see p.117
Sprouting broccoli	see p.137
Summer carrots	see p.50
Sweetcorn	see p.145
Tomatoes	see p.149

Prioritise the transformers

Garlic, chillies and herbs may be delicious in their own right, but their great gift is in offering other crops any number of costumes to dress up in, transforming great harvests into outstanding meals.

Summer carrots, brushed clean and munched straight out of the soil, may be as sweet as it gets, but your winter harvest will shift a couple of notches up the culinary ladder with the addition of rosemary or coriander. What makes a tomato seem even more tomatoey? Basil. And where do you start with the wonderful contribution garlic makes to any number of dishes? And think visually too – edible flowers, with their colour as much as their flavour, add a punctuating spike to any number of salads.

For the most part, the transformers are expensive to buy, yet easy to grow, taking up very little of your precious space, so make room for as many as you can – they'll multiply your kitchen possibilities endlessly.

Top 5 transformers

Garlic	see p.81
Herbs	see p.87
Chilli peppers	see p.65
Edible flowers	see p.72
Shallots and spring onions	see p.128 and p.135

Prioritise the most 'expensive' foods

Growing your own is as much about old chestnuts as it is about new shoots, and one standard line that you can fairly well rely on is that by the time you've factored in your time, growing your own may well not be the most rewarding economic activity. But that doesn't mean it can't knock a fair-sized hole in your weekly shop or save you the expense of that gym membership. Check through the veg you buy across all four seasons and identify the most expensive – many are surprisingly easy to grow, and are often expensive only because they are limited to a short period of production, or are tricky to harvest on a commercial scale. Asparagus is a classic, commanding a high price, yet requiring little more than planting once and keeping reasonably free of weeds.

Top 5 money savers

Asparagus	see p.28
Globe artichokes	see p.85
Sprouting broccoli	see p.137
Most herbs	see p.87
New potatoes	see p.117

Cut down on food miles

Growing everything we eat may not be a realistic option for all of us, but putting a sizeable dent in your food-related carbon emissions may be easier than you think. Growing your food organically is the biggest step you can make in reducing your food's footprint, but there is a little extra targeting that can make all the difference in greening up your larder. If you enjoy fruit normally sourced overseas (like peaches and apricots) climate change is making it easier to grow them here in the UK, but bizarrely many of the veg we import the most can also be grown here with ease. Green beans and peas top the list, so if you like them, grow them for yourself.

Top 5 imported veg

French beans	see p.79
Peas	see p.110
Sweetcorn	see p.145
Asparagus	see p.28
Onions	see p.102

Grow something beautiful

A beautiful plot is a more enticing place to spend your time. Make room for some flowers, some are edible (see p.72), many suit cutting for the house, and most will bring beneficial insects to your patch and encourage the biodiversity that should underpin any piece of the planet, however small.

A good-looking plot doesn't necessarily equate to neatness, and everyone's idea of what is pleasing to the eye is unique, but nurture your own sense of the beautiful and your patch will become the place you most want to be for your morning coffee, to read your Sunday paper, or to sip that early-evening cider. And every time you're there – even if you're not gardening – you'll notice something, attend to something small, pick up on progress, and get to nibble at the emerging harvests.

Top 5 ornamental veg

Globe artichokes	see p.85
Jerusalem artichokes	see p.92
Runner beans	see p.124
Borlotti beans	see p.36
Florence fennel	see p.76

Get some seed catalogues

Catalogues aren't just the source of your seeds – they're the inspiration for trying new foods, different varieties, and for stirring up anticipation through the colder months. Get on the internet, check the directory (p.265) for catalogue suppliers and nose around – they're not all the same. Many specialise, and (as with anything) prices and quality will vary, so it pays to invest a little time reading a few through the winter.

Essential tools

If you've ever tried putting up a shelf you'll be familiar with the spirit-sapping tedium that comes with poor-quality tools. Think of them as an investment – spend your money well and they'll pay you back for years, take short cuts and you'll regret it every time you pick them up. Take time to try some, ask around, borrow a few and buy them for how they feel in your hands and how they perform in the soil, not for how they look.

There are a few tools that you simply shouldn't be without:

A fork This is the workhorse of your veg patch, used to loosen or break up ground as well as for lifting your root crops. Get your hands on a good one before you buy any other tools.

A spade For digging, cutting straight edges, and turning compost.

A hoe For weeding between plants or larger areas. Some work by pushing, others by pulling – try some out before you buy as you'll have your hoe in your hands a fair bit. At the same time, get a sharpening stone – it will save you endless energy.

A rake For levelling and working the surface of your patch. Go for a sturdy rake rather than one of those spindly things designed for collecting leaves.

A trowel and a hand fork These let you get in close to dig small areas for planting into and spot-weeding. They'll be in your hand more than any other tools – so make sure they feel comfortable – and if you can stretch to it, get a couple of spares for those times you have extra help.

A wheelbarrow, watering can and two buckets are also indispensable. The rest of the items you might need can be homemade – a line of string between sticks makes as straight a guideline for planting as anything, and you can use a sturdy stick to make holes for dropping your leeks into rather than use a dibber.

The cost can mount up, so do investigate second-hand shops, car boot sales, the local recycling centre, and the possibility of sharing tools. And there are always the on-line auction sites. Some good starting places in your search are included in the directory (pp.265–6).

Essential terms

Growing, like most things, has its fair share of jargon – much of which can obscure rather than illuminate. Most terms are explained as you come across them in the book, but it's worth being familiar with the following as they crop up regularly.

Annual An annual plant is a plant that germinates, flowers and dies (or is harvested before it dies) in one year.

Biennial A biennial plant takes two years to complete its life-cycle.

Blanching As far as the veg patch is concerned, blanching refers to the exclusion of light (usually intentionally) from parts of a plant, with the aim of producing a more succulent, sweeter crop.

In the kitchen, blanching describes the brief boiling of vegetables (for a minute or so) before plunging into cold water, in order to arrest the conversion of sugars to starch and/or retain maximum texture. Vegetables are usually blanched before freezing.

Cut-and-come-again Some vegetables, such as lettuces, do not have to be grown to full maturity. Instead, you can harvest their leaves by cutting or picking, after which the plant will keep growing to give you further harvests. The main advantages are that harvesting in this way avoids gluts, makes harvesting mixed leaves in usable quantities easier, and you can get a longer, steadier harvest from a small space.

Cut-and-come-again

F1 varieties/F1 hybrids These are the result of a cross between two distinct varieties. Many F1s offer vigorous, predictable, disease-resistant and high-yielding plants. The disadvantages include the higher cost of seeds, the fact that the seed is not worth saving as new plants will be weak at best, and that all your F1 seeds of the same variety tend to mature simultaneously – the home-grower usually aims for a more gradual harvest.

Forcing The process of accelerating growth, usually by increasing the temperature and/or light manipulation. The aim is usually either to get an earlier crop and/or a sweeter, less bitter one.

Hardening off If you've started off any plants under cover, most seedlings will adjust much more quickly to life in your veg patch if you give them the chance to acclimatise first. To do this, move your seedlings outside in the morning, taking them back under cover for night. This is usually done for 4 or 5 days for vegetables, and is the process known as hardening off.

Perennial A perennial plant is a plant that lives for more than two years.

Pollination Before a plant can bear fruit and create seed, its flowers need pollinating. This involves the transfer of pollen from the anther (a structure at the tip of the stamen where pollen is produced) to the stigma. Self-fertile plants can do this themselves using their own pollen. Others require pollination from another variety of the same plant.

Potting on The process of moving your seedlings to a larger pot, to ensure they have sufficient space for the roots to develop unhindered.

Running to seed/bolting This is when a plant begins to try to form seeds; usually accompanied by rapid formation of flowers. It is generally triggered by a cold spell, or by changes in day length, or by an extended dry period.

Sowing direct To sow seeds straight into the soil rather than start them off in modules etc.

Sowing under cover To sow seeds in a polytunnel, greenhouse, or even on a windowsill, in order to protect from pests and/or provide more warmth.

Tilth Refers to the condition and texture of the soil surface – usually a 'good tilth' implies an even, fine texture into which you can sow seed.

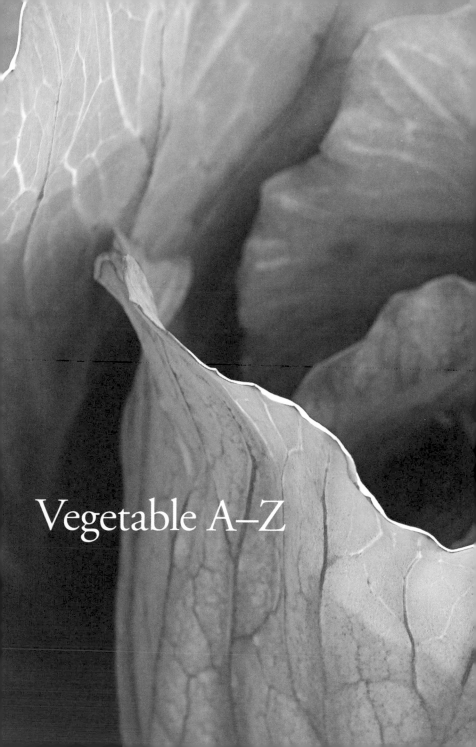

Vegetable A–Z

I've included all the vegetables, herbs and edible flowers that I love, and a few even that I just quite like. Inevitably there are some that didn't make the cut for one reason or another – okra is too unreliable for most people here in the UK, oka (a South American tuber) is lovely, but hard to source. Don't let this stand in your way of adding more to your wish list. Seed catalogues, on-line forums, blogs and cookbooks are great sources of inspiration – you're bound to find another food you want to try and any number of varieties worth giving a go.

Sowing times are included as a guide – they can vary considerably depending on whether you live in the Highlands or High Wycombe, and of course from year to year. The seasons are delightfully fluid – I am no more able to name the date that I expect the first frost here than I can tell you when it will come where you are. But it's not worth getting too hung up on. If it says to sow in early March but it's unseasonably cold, leave it a week or two. The essential thing is not to worry about getting it right all the time, but to do it. You'll learn as much from what doesn't work out as what does, and you'll develop a feel for it surprisingly quickly.

If you want to push the odds slightly more in your favour, then you can start many plants off under cover – in a polytunnel, under a cloche or even on a windowsill. Where this is possible, I've included times for sowing under cover – along with an idea of when these seedlings should be moved outside for planting.

You can grow many plants all the way through to harvest under cover if you are fortunate enough to have a polytunnel or greenhouse. Both take the edge off the outside temperatures and allow you not only a head start in getting things under way, but also a few precious weeks at the end of the summer to ripen things fully. It's a pretty reliable rule that you can sow direct in a polytunnel a month or so earlier than you can outside, and harvest a month or so longer than you can outside. In some cases, you'll even be able to coax a year-round supply in this protected space where it would be impossible to do so outside. Bear this in mind when reading the sowing times.

I have also included an idea of how to get to grips with each of the foods when they reach your kitchen, and suggested particular ways to prepare and cook them that I think show them off at their best. If you are unfamiliar with any of the foods then this should give you a good approach to trying them out. But that's just the start – be adventurous, play around with different vegetables and get the most from your harvests.

You'll come across plenty of sources of inspiration. Talking of which, I'd really recommend you invest in Pam Corbin's *River Cottage Preserves Handbook*. In many ways, the art of preserving is the final step on that perfect journey that begins in the soil and ends at your table. Get yourself familiar with the many ways of arresting the process of decay and you'll not only stretch your harvest further, you'll have even more reminders of why it was all worth it.

Vegetable sowing, planting and harvesting times

	JAN	FEB	MARCH	APRIL	MAY	JUNE	JULY	AUG	SEPT	OCT	NOV	DEC
ASPARAGUS												
Start under cover		•										
Plant out			•	•								
Harvest					•	•						
AUBERGINES												
Start under cover		•	•									
Plant out					•	•						
Harvest								•	•	•		
BEETROOT												
Start under cover			•	•	•							
Plant out				•	•	•						
Sow direct				•	•	•	•					
Harvest							•	•	•	•		
BORLOTTI BEANS												
Start under cover			•	•	•	•	•					
Plant out					•	•	•					
Sow direct				•	•	•	•					
Harvest								•	•	•		
BROAD BEANS												
Start under cover		•	•	•								
Plant out				•	•	•	•					
Sow direct				•							•	
Harvest				•	•	•	•	•	•			
BRUSSELS SPROUTS												
Start under cover		•	•	•								
Plant out					•	•						
Harvest	•	•	•	•						•	•	•
CABBAGES (summer/autumn harvest)												
Start under cover			•	•								
Plant out					•	•						
Harvest						•	•	•	•	•		
CABBAGES (winter harvest)												
Start under cover			•	•								
Plant out						•	•					
Harvest	•	•	•								•	•
CABBAGES (spring harvest)												
Start under cover							•	•				
Plant out									•	•		
Harvest			•	•	•	•						
CALABRESE												
Start under cover			•	•	•							
Plant out				•	•	•						
Sow direct			•	•	•							
Harvest						•	•	•	•			

	JAN	FEB	MARCH	APRIL	MAY	JUNE	JULY	AUG	SEPT	OCT	NOV	DEC
CARDOONS												
Start under cover			•	•								
Plant out					•	•						
Harvest										•	•	
CARROTS												
Sow direct			•	•	•	•						
Harvest						•	•	•	•	•	•	
CAULIFLOWERS (summer harvest)												
Start under cover	•	•	•									
Plant out			•	•	•							
Harvest						•	•	•	•	•	•	
CAULIFLOWERS (winter harvest)												
Start under cover				•	•	•	•					
Plant out						•	•	•	•			
Harvest	•	•	•	•	•						•	•
CELERIAC												
Start under cover		•	•									
Plant out					•	•						
Harvest	•	•	•						•	•	•	•
CELERY												
Start under cover		•	•									
Plant out					•	•						
Harvest								•	•	•		
CHARD & PERPETUAL SPINACH												
Start under cover			•	•	•	•	•	•	•			
Plant out				•	•	•	•	•	•	•		
Sow direct				•	•	•	•	•				
Harvest	•	•	•	•	•	•	•	•	•	•	•	•
CHICORY												
Sow direct					•	•	•					
Harvest	•									•	•	•
CHILLI PEPPERS												
Start under cover		•	•	•								
Plant out						•						
Harvest								•	•	•		
COURGETTES												
Start under cover				•	•	•						
Plant out					•	•	•					
Harvest							•	•	•	•		
CUCUMBERS & GHERKINS												
Start under cover			•	•	•							
Plant out					•	•						
Harvest							•	•	•	•		
ENDIVE												
Sow direct					•	•	•	•				
Harvest	•	•	•					•	•	•	•	•
FLORENCE FENNEL												
Sow direct				•	•	•	•					
Harvest						•	•	•	•	•	•	

	JAN	FEB	MARCH	APRIL	MAY	JUNE	JULY	AUG	SEPT	OCT	NOV	DEC
FRENCH BEANS												
Start under cover			•	•	•	•	•					
Plant out					•	•	•	•				
Sow direct				•	•	•	•					
Harvest					•	•	•	•	•	•		
GARLIC												
Sow direct		•	•							•	•	
Harvest						•	•	•	•	•		
GLOBE ARTICHOKES												
Start under cover		•	•									
Plant out						•	•					
Harvest						•	•	•	•	•		
JERUSALEM ARTICHOKES												
Sow direct	•	•	•									
Harvest	•	•	•							•	•	•
KALE												
Start under cover			•	•	•	•	•	•				
Plant out				•	•	•	•	•	•			
Harvest	•	•				•	•	•	•	•	•	•
LEEKS												
Start under cover		•	•	•								
Plant out						•	•					
Harvest	•	•	•	•	•				•	•	•	•
LETTUCES												
Start under cover	•	•	•	•	•	•	•	•	•			
Plant out				•	•	•	•	•	•	•		
Sow direct			•	•	•	•	•	•	•			
Harvest	•	•	•	•	•	•	•	•	•	•	•	•
ONIONS												
Sow direct			•	•					•	•		
Harvest						•	•	•	•	•		
PARSNIPS												
Sow direct			•	•	•							
Harvest	•	•	•					•	•	•	•	•
PEAS												
Start under cover		•	•	•	•							
Plant out						•	•					
Sow direct			•	•	•	•				•	•	
Harvest						•	•	•	•	•		
PEPPERS												
Start under cover		•	•									
Plant out						•	•					
Harvest									•	•	•	•
POTATOES												
Sow direct		•	•	•								
Harvest						•	•	•	•	•		
RADISHES												
Sow direct			•	•	•	•	•	•				
Harvest				•	•	•	•	•	•	•	•	

	JAN	FEB	MARCH	APRIL	MAY	JUNE	JULY	AUG	SEPT	OCT	NOV	DEC
ROCKET												
Sow direct			•	•	•	•	•	•	•			
Harvest				•	•	•	•	•	•	•	•	
RUNNER BEANS												
Start under cover				•	•	•						
Plant out					•	•	•					
Sow direct				•	•							
Harvest						•	•	•	•	•		
SALSIFY & SCORZONERA												
Sow direct				•	•							
Harvest										•	•	
SHALLOTS												
Sow direct		•	•									
Harvest								•	•	•		
SORREL												
Sow direct				•	•							
Harvest						•	•	•	•	•	•	
SPINACH												
Sow direct				•	•	•	•	•	•	•		
Harvest	•	•	•	•	•	•	•	•	•	•	•	•
SPRING ONIONS												
Sow direct		•	•	•	•	•	•	•		•	•	
Harvest	•	•	•	•	•	•	•	•	•	•	•	
SPROUTING BROCCOLI												
Start under cover				•	•							
Plant out						•	•					
Sow direct				•	•							
Harvest	•	•	•	•								
SQUASH, PUMPKINS & GOURDS												
Start under cover				•	•	•						
Plant out						•	•					
Harvest										•	•	
SWEDE												
Sow direct				•	•	•						
Harvest	•	•							•	•	•	•
SWEETCORN												
Start under cover				•								
Plant out					•	•						
Sow direct					•							
Harvest								•	•	•		
TOMATOES												
Start under cover		•	•									
Plant out				•	•	•						
Harvest								•	•	•	•	
TURNIPS												
Sow direct			•	•	•	•	•					
Harvest						•	•	•	•	•		

Asparagus *Asparagus officinalis*

PLANT GROUP	Perennials (see p.169)
START UNDER COVER	February
PLANT OUT	Seedlings: June; Crowns: March–April
HARVEST	May–June

The arrival of spring and the warming soil promise so much, yet I can't help feeling impatient at this time of the year as it's still the best part of a month until the first asparagus appears. I suffer from what food writer Simon Hopkinson calls 'asparagus fever'. Obsessively, I check for their emerging green noses every morning and most afternoons from April Fools' Day. When those tips eventually do break the surface, it feels like the new season's harvest is really getting under way and about to offer one of the finest flavours a veg patch can provide. How fitting that it comes first in the A–Z... if it hadn't I'd have considered misspelling it 'aasparagus'.

Be prepared to develop the addiction once you've tasted asparagus fresh from the ground. Fortunately, in Britain we have the ideal conditions for producing the finest there is, so do grow some and chill some good dry white wine in anticipation.

Varieties

'Connover's Colossal' and 'Mary Washington' are older varieties that produce good yields of particularly delicious spears. Plants can be male or female, with the former tending to give greater overall yield, the latter usually producing larger spears.

The newer F1 varieties, such as 'Jersey Knight', produce all-male plants so the harvest is likely to be larger and more uniform. However, I prefer using non-F1s and the variety in size that comes with them.

How to grow

Asparagus can be raised from seed (sown in modules in February for transplanting in June), but most people go for young dormant plants known as crowns. Being a year older, they cost more, but the reward of an earlier crop justifies the price.

Growing asparagus is easy. Choose a well-drained site, or raise the bed if you've slightly heavier soil, and dig up any perennial weeds. In late March or early April, dig a trench to a spade's depth, incorporating a little compost or well-rotted manure into the bottom. Shovel in around 10cm of soil and mound this up into a ridge at the bottom of the trench. Space the crowns at least 50cm apart along the ridge and spread the roots out evenly on either side. Cover the crowns with 10cm or so of soil and water well. Allow about 80cm between rows. If you cover the rows with a mulch of grass cuttings or manure you'll help to retain moisture and suppress weeds.

Asparagus 'Mary Washington'

There's usually one stage where a vegetable needs a little extra attention. With asparagus this comes early and involves keeping the bed weed-free, as asparagus hates competition. This is best done by hand as hoeing damages the shallow roots. In autumn, when the foliage yellows, cut the stems back to 5cm above the soil. A tip I learnt from Ray Smith (the River Cottage butcher) is to support plant rows with a ring of string. Simply place canes along either side of the lines of asparagus and link them with a loop of string – this prevents a hole forming at the base of the plant as it sways in the wind, where water can get in and rot the roots.

That's it – that's all that stands between you and just about the finest lunch you could wish for. After that, barring a little self-restraint in the first years, it's slippery chins every May and June.

How to harvest

Sit on your hands, go on holiday in May, do whatever you have to, but don't take spears in the first 2 years, or 3 years if growing from seed. The plant needs the top growth to direct energies towards getting a root system established.

After that, clear a space in your diary for when the asparagus spears break the surface as May approaches. When they reach 15cm or so, use a bread knife (or a specialist asparagus knife) to cut them a couple of centimetres below the surface. Stop harvesting by the longest day.

Carefully tended, asparagus plants should crop for 20 years or more, with each crown yielding around 10 spears each season.

Problems and pests

Asparagus beetle can be a nuisance, but is easy to spot with its black and white back and distinctive red rim. If the beetle (or its larvae) shows itself, simply pick off and squash them, or feed them to the chickens.

How to eat

Enjoying asparagus is not so much about recipes as it is about time. Seconds seem to matter, minutes definitely do. It's no exaggeration to say that if you have the water boiling before you cut the spears you'll notice the difference. Just boil or steam your spears within seconds of picking and enjoy with butter, salt, black pepper and Parmesan, or with hollandaise sauce (see p.258). Hugh's soft-boiled egg accompaniment is delicious, and there is something very satisfying about the scruff-meets-toff of asparagus soldiers with soft-boiled eggs.

Most other recipes are based on the assumption that you will tire of eating asparagus simply (as above), which I think is nonsense, but if you've a genuine glut they will take happily to a gratin (see p.127), and make a delicately flavoured houmous (see p.229). For more recipes, see pp.244, 248, 250.

Aubergines *Solanum melongena*

PLANT GROUP	Solanaceae (see p.168)
START UNDER COVER	February–March
PLANT OUT	May–June
HARVEST	August–October

Along with courgettes and sweetcorn, aubergines make up the holy trinity of barbecue veg. Maybe it's those oily griddle lines that cart your mind off to the Med, but they are a must when the charcoal comes out.

Shop-bought aubergines rarely offer much in the way of flavour, yet home-grown, they have a real creaminess with a finer flavour. It does, however, take a little effort to ensure a late-summer harvest. Aubergines like sun and are comparatively easily knocked off their steady course to maturity, so grow them under cover and take out a little edible insurance. I start some in the polytunnel, some on windowsills, and I still sow a second batch a couple of weeks later as a backup.

Varieties
Most varieties are indistinguishable in taste, apart from 'Moneymaker' (F1), which is particularly delicious, and the beautiful 'Rosa Bianca', which is creamier than most. 'Black Beauty' is a very dependable cropper. 'Slim Jim' is a slender, smaller-fruiting variety that needs less ripening, so should give you more chance of a crop if you live in the North or are growing them in containers.

How to grow
I start aubergines off under cover in Jiffy 7s (see p.197) or modules in March, potting on regularly as they grow. Get them into the soil under cover (in a polytunnel or cloche) in May, or if you're an optimist outside in June. Attention to detail is vital in swinging the odds of a good harvest your way. Add some good compost before planting, and remember that growing them in a polytunnel, greenhouse or on a windowsill is likely to offer your best chance of success.

Support the plant as it grows by tying it to a sturdy cane. Take care when weeding or picking as the stems are easily damaged. Fortnightly comfrey or seaweed feeds (see p.215) from immediately after flowering will help to bring the fruit to its peak.

How to harvest
Expect to harvest from August through until mid-October. Don't wait until the aubergines reach supermarket proportions – snip them off any time after they get to 8cm in length (and up to 18cm or so) to get them at their best.

Aubergine flower

Aubergine 'Black Beauty'

Problems and pests

Apart from a less than belting summer, aphids and red spider mites are likely to be the main obstacles between you and tasty late-summer aubergines. Try companion planting with basil (see p.212), rubbing off any aphids that appear. If you still find your plants under attack then parasitic controls are the best solution, see the directory (pp.265–6) for suppliers.

How to eat

Aubergines are perfect sliced, brushed with olive oil and griddled on the barbecue. Cut them into slightly larger pieces and they also take well to roasting.

Aubergine caviar makes a delicious dip or topping for toast. Top and tail a few aubergines and boil them until tender. Drain in a colander and let them dry out and cool a little before peeling. Mash the flesh with a little lemon juice, olive oil and salt and pepper to taste, then serve warm.

Although not essential, before cooking, you can salt your aubergine slices for half an hour, then rinse and pat them dry with a clean tea towel or kitchen paper. This removes any hint of bitterness, which is absent in most newer varieties, but also reduces the amount of oil they take up, allowing their delicate flavour to shine through. For more recipes, see pp.248, 256.

Beetroot *Beta vulgaris*

PLANT GROUP	Roots (see p.162)
START UNDER COVER	March–June
PLANT OUT	May–July
SOW DIRECT	April–July
HARVEST	July–October

I'm still mystified as to why carrots are so much more popular than beetroot. Both plants give up deliciously sweet, versatile, easy-to-grow roots, yet beetroot also has outstanding leaves, heavy with vitamin A to go with the vitamin C-rich beets. And this isn't one of those veg where the root is the prize and the leaves merely edible. Swiss chard is the same plant – bred to swell at the stem rather than the root, so rest assured of a quality double harvest.

Sow beetroot early in the spring and you'll have tender, sweet salad leaves before the summer arrives, followed by purple marbles to crunch raw through the hottest months, and snooker-ball-sized globes to boil or roast as the heat starts to dip off in the autumn. Sow them successionally and you can even have the three-stage harvest at once.

Naturally, we associate beetroot with the familiar ruby-red swollen roots, but there are also golden, white and candy-striped varieties, which can be cooked and eaten in much the same way.

As with carrots or fennel, beetroot offers so much more than just a side-veg supporting role – happily transforming any course from the canapés through to puddings. If you're growing beetroot for the first time, try some of the recipe ideas (see p.35) and prepare for them to take over your kitchen.

Varieties

'Barabietola di Chioggia' is a traditional, hard-to-beat beet with wonderful concentric pink and white circles within. This Italian favourite is good grated raw, but really comes into its own once cooked, when it turns particularly sweet. If you are after the longest season, 'Egyptian Turnip Rooted' and 'Pronto' are early varieties which don't easily run to seed. Both have outstanding leaves for salad, and roots that take very happily to the roasting tin, as well as being outstanding raw.

I've also grown 'Moneta' this year for the first time and it's been excellent for both beets and leaves. For added aesthetics as well as top-drawer flavour, try sowing a row of 'Burpees Golden', adding the sweetly delicious golden beets to any recipe to contrast with their purple cousins.

Beetroot 'Barabietola di Chioggia'

How to grow

I sow early beetroot under cover in modules in March for planting out around 6 weeks later, but the majority I sow direct from April through to July. Sowing every few weeks will ensure a successional crop.

Space and size are yours to play with. Give them more room and you'll get larger beets; give them less and you'll have more, but smaller, beets from your veg patch. I prefer not to sit around tending to swollen prize-winning veg – we are growing them for the table rather than the local show after all. So, I pull them when they are golf-ball- to snooker-ball-sized. I still tend to sow reasonably close though, thinning them gradually to 8cm apart and taking the young plants to use in the kitchen. The rows should be around 20cm apart.

How to harvest

The smallest plants make delicious raw, leafy throw-ins to salads, with anything that has more than a marble of beetroot worth a few minutes of steaming. Expect the main harvest around 3 months after sowing.

If, as many people do, you find you've sown too many and your harvest is too large, leave some to grow on over winter. They'll look fantastic and give you a fine hungry-gap harvest of new leaves.

Problems and pests

If birds nipping at leaves or seeds are a pain, do whatever works best for you – CDs swinging in the wind, netting, scarecrows, falconry, blunderbuss...

How to eat

Beetroot is incredibly versatile. The young leaves are perfect in salads, and when they're a little larger and coarser, you can steam them like spinach. The roots make a wonderful houmous (see p.229). When roasted or boiled, they transform into sweet tender globes. They also make a delicious substitute for potatoes in a gratin dauphinoise, and a perfect alternative for their orange cousins in carrot cake. Sweet and earthy, beetroot has a particular affinity with soft cheese (especially goat's cheese), garlic and thyme.

Roast or boil them in their skins with a few centimetres of the leaves and all of the roots on – this prevents the sweet purpley juices leaching out. The result is sweeter, more tender and somehow more 'beetroot' – its very essence magnified. Leave until cool enough to handle before peeling.

For more recipes, see pp.223, 233, 240, 242, 260.

Borlotti beans *Phaseolus vulgaris*

PLANT GROUP	Legumes (see p.157)
START UNDER COVER	March–July
PLANT OUT	May–July
SOW DIRECT	April–July
HARVEST	August–October

Borlottis are worth growing for the beauty of their stunning speckled pods alone, but the beans also happen to be luscious and versatile. Although superficially similar to kidney beans, their red and cream speckle, finer texture and sweeter flavour set them apart. You can use them fresh in salads or on toast, dried in earthy winter stews and soups, or save them for next season's sowing. They are rarely available to anyone but the home-grower, so give them some space – and yourself a treat.

Varieties
'Lingua di Fuoco' is reliable, delicious and the most widely available variety.

How to grow
Start borlotti seeds under cover from March until early July for an autumn harvest; root trainers (see p.197) allow their roots to develop well. Let them get to at least 5cm tall before planting out, from mid-May. You can also sow seeds direct from late April until early July. Most varieties are climbers and will require a tepee or other structure to support them as they grow. They love the sun, so give them a good light site, with around 20cm between plants. And keep them well watered from flowering onwards, using comfrey tea (see p.215) every other week to promote a longer harvest.

How to harvest
The main harvest is August and September, but if you are after a long season, early and successional sowings can stretch this from June to November. Pick borlottis when the pods begin to turn cream – you can always pop one if you're unsure.

For dried beans or seed saving for next year, leave the beans in place until the weather is about to turn wet, then cut the plant and hang it upside down somewhere light and airy until the pods really desiccate. Next, shell the beans and allow them to dry for a few more days on paper, before storing in a paper bag or airproof jar.

Problems and pests
Marigolds (*Tagetes* sp.) are a good companion plant, deterring aphids and attracting the ladybirds and hoverflies that will finish off any aphids that do appear. Starting

borlottis (or any legume) under cover is the best way to minimise the impact of slugs and snails, but be prepared for slug-picking duty every other evening.

How to eat

Borlotti beans are lovely dried, but get them fresh and they are softer, slightly more flavoursome and cook more quickly. They have that rare quality of taking on other flavours yet being distinctive enough to shine on their own or alongside saltier sheep's and goat's cheeses. Robust in texture, they are ideal in stews and soups, but also suit a softer approach – try borlotti houmous (see p.229). Once dried, they are usually soaked overnight before cooking. Be aware that cooking tends to fade the speckles. For more recipes, see pp.223, 230, 248.

Borlotti beans 'Lingua di Fuoca'

Broad bean 'Aquadulce Claudia'

Broad beans *Vicia faba*

PLANT GROUP	Legumes (see p.157)
START UNDER COVER	February–May
PLANT OUT	April–July
SOW DIRECT	November or April
HARVEST	April–September

Take a mid-spring trip to Worth Matravers in Dorset and follow the footpath that loops east from the pub before turning south to meet the cliffs. Head west, following the coastline for a mile or two, turning inland at the signpost before you reach Chapman's Pool. Here, if you're lucky, you'll find a full field of broad beans in flower. Hold your breath and walk quickly to the centre, then close your eyes and breathe in the loveliest, most intoxicating perfume there is.

While their perfume is indisputably superb, broad beans themselves seem to divide people into believers and detractors, with few sitting on the fence. I'm firmly with the believers. This is one of those prime harvests that really must be home-grown to be enjoyed at its peak. If you are one of those unfortunates that doesn't like broad beans, I'm convinced it is just that you don't like them yet. Indeed, you are one of the fortunates. How wonderful to have the revelation of just-picked, just-cooked broad beans as a discovery to come. I'm genuinely envious.

Varieties

Offering delectable, reliable harvests, 'Bunyards Exhibition' and 'Green Windsor' are hard to beat for springtime sowing. With their long pods filled with so many small, tender beans, 'Aquadulce Claudia' is the best for autumn sowings. 'The Sutton' is a good hardy dwarf variety, which grows half a metre high and does well in a fairly exposed site. It will even give a decent crop when grown in large pots.

How to grow

I start most of mine off under cover, in toilet roll inners or root trainers (see p.197), every 3 weeks from late February through to the end of May, to plant out a month later. This successional sowing gives a nice steady harvest from late May onwards.

If you want a slightly earlier harvest, you can sow broad beans direct in November (ready to harvest in April), but be prepared for birds, mice and the wet to deplete any direct-sown seed.

Sow or plant the seedlings 20cm apart, 5cm deep, and in rows 60cm apart. You'll need to pinch out the top few centimetres of growth on the main stem when the flowers have just wilted and the first pods are starting to appear. This directs energy to the developing pods and (as this is their favourite part) reduces the likelihood of aphid infestations. Taller varieties may need supporting with a hoop of string around canes placed along each side of your rows and at row ends. Water the beans through any dry periods.

How to harvest

If you sow in November you may get your first beans in late April, otherwise expect to be picking around 3 months after you've sown your seeds in spring and summer. Before cooking you'll need to remove the beans from the pods. Allow for the beans to be around a third of the weight of the unopened pods.

Problems and pests

Keep a watch for ants on your plants. They won't be causing any harm, but they are there for a reason – looking for aphids. Aphids secrete honeydew, which the ants can detect in minute amounts, so if you see them it may be that your broad beans are about to come under attack from the aphid militia. Get your spray hose ready. Better still, if you have a few nettles growing nearby, leave them. You may find, as I do, that they work as a perfect sacrificial plant, drawing almost all of the aphids to them and away from your precious pods.

Pea and bean weevil may leave its characteristic notches in the foliage, but damage is cosmetic. As is chocolate spot, looking as the name implies. Good air circulation and keeping your plants watered through dry patches helps minimise the likelihood of this fungal disease.

How to eat

Broad beans are as versatile as it gets – happy with most fresh herbs, lemon juice and many of the saltier cheeses like feta, sheep's or goat's cheese. The perfect spring beans on toast, they also lend themselves to endless salads, and make a wonderful alternative in the houmous recipe (see p.229).

Generally, you'll be looking to give them a couple of minutes in simmering water to bring out maximum sweetness. But it's not only freshness that makes the home-grown haul so superior to the shop-bought; they are simply that much more delicious eaten young and smaller than a thumbnail. Get them early enough and they are even wonderful raw. Do try steaming whole pods when small (no more than a few centimetres) for a few minutes. Later-season beans can run with stronger flavours, such as garlic and ginger. And if broad beans are particularly large, slip them out of their skins, as these are likely to be a bit tough.

Don't discard the leafy pinched-out tops. One of the top treats for the greedy gardener, they are fantastic in risotto, as a steamed side dish or wilted in butter.

For more recipes, see pp.226, 230, 244, 248, 251.

Brussels sprouts

Brassica oleracea var. *gemmifera*

PLANT GROUP	Brassicas (see p.159)
START UNDER COVER	February–April
PLANT OUT	May–June
HARVEST	October–April

We think of Brussels sprouts as Christmas veg on a stick, yet by growing a few different varieties, you can enjoy these wonderfully nutty nuggets for around 3 months either side of the festive season. I can't get enough of them, but for some reason, sprouts seem to split the nation: you either love them or loathe them. Perhaps as a child you were, quite rightly, repelled by them being overcooked. The characteristic house-filling sulphurous smell that results is enough to put anyone off. Put aside any preconceptions that you might have and try boiling or steaming sprouts lightly instead. Discover their friendship with cream, nuts and bacon, and you'll surely start to enjoy them.

Varieties

'Noisette' and 'Groninger' are outstanding pre-Christmas sprouts, with 'Seven Hills' taking you through the festive season. 'Wellington' and 'Red Rubine' (with its wonderful deep-red sprouts) will give you a fine late winter harvest.

How to grow

Growing Brussels sprouts requires a touch of patience, but very little in the way of effort. Start them off under cover in pots or Jiffy 7s (see p.197) as winter turns to spring, then plant them out about 60cm apart as spring becomes summer when they are around 10–15cm tall. The plants are shallow-rooting yet tall, so firm them in really well, and tread the bed over.

To make the most of the space, you can always squeeze in a few fast-maturing salad leaves, radishes or leafy herbs around the base of the plants, to give you a quick harvest before the Brussels sprouts grow to any size.

Planting early and later varieties of sprouts, which mature at different rates, will ensure a harvest from October through to Easter. Check the catalogue or seed packet for planting and harvesting times.

Brussels sprouts require little in the way of care while they are getting up to size. Just keep an eye out for pests that show interest, and water the plants during an extended dry period.

Brussels sprouts 'Wellington'

How to harvest

With its tight nobbles dotted along its chunky stem and an umbrella of rubbery leaves, you could be forgiven for wondering which part of the plant is destined for the kitchen. It's those mini-cabbages along the stalk that are your primary prize, but don't neglect the leaves. These make fine cut-and-come-again greens, often tasting milder than the sprouts themselves. Take just a few at a time and leave the rest for the plant.

If you're after all the sprouts on a plant at once, chop the top of the plant off in October and, for some mysterious reason, they'll all mature together for Christmas (fingers crossed). Otherwise, leave the top on and nip the sprouts off as they mature. And if you have chickens, hang the leftover stalks upside down, as they make fine edible pecking posts.

Problems and pests

Cabbage white caterpillars and slugs will almost certainly try to beat you to your harvest. Picking them off is the most effective remedy (see pp.216–17 for other methods). Pigeons will either bother your veg patch intensely or not at all. Be prepared to net against them, string CDs up to swing in the wind and flash reflected light, or look up a good pigeon pie recipe.

How to eat

Steaming sprouts should only take around 6 minutes or so, unless they are large in which case they'll need longer. As with any green leafy vegetable, add them to a pan containing plenty of well-salted boiling water and cook until just tender, then drain and serve at once. Or, once cooked, immediately plunge them into cold water to retain that lively green colour, then drain; reheat in a pan with a little butter when ready to serve.

Sprouts tossed in a little melted butter or olive oil are a truly delicious side veg. And any that don't get eaten will be perfect sliced and combined with other veg to make bubble and squeak.

You can dress sprouts up with any number of partners. Once steamed, push them around a pan with melted butter, seasoned with salt, pepper and nutmeg, before serving with grated Parmesan. They will take to various other flavourings: lemon, almonds, garlic, chives, peppercorns are all worth playing around with. However, my favourite way to eat Brussels sprouts is creamed with chestnuts and bacon (see p. 255).

Cabbages *Brassica oleracea* var. *capitata*

PLANT GROUP	Brassicas (see p.159)
START UNDER COVER	Summer/autumn cabbages: March–April Winter cabbages: April–May Spring cabbages: July–August
PLANT OUT	Around 6 weeks after sowing, when 7 or 8cm tall
HARVEST	Year round, depending on variety:– Summer/autumn cabbages: June–October Winter cabbages: November–March Spring cabbages: March–June

You could be forgiven for thinking that cabbages are a pretty ordinary bunch, with the limited range on offer in supermarkets. But grow your own and you'll soon appreciate how diverse and delicious they are, and how choice of variety is critical to enjoying them at their finest. For visual as well as culinary impact, varieties such as 'Red Drumhead' and 'January King' are up there with any ornamental plant.

You'll find cabbage varieties for harvesting throughout the year. However, much as I love them, I grow few cabbages through the summer because I don't want them to crowd out too much of my valuable plot through the busier, sunnier months.

Varieties

For summer and autumn harvesting: 'Red Drumhead', which is tasty and stunning to look at, is a must. 'Marner Early Red' is another beautiful red cabbage, excellent raw. 'Greyhound' is a reliable, flavoursome green summer cabbage.

For winter harvesting: 'Cuor di Bue', 'January King' and 'Best of All' (the finest Savoy) cannot be equalled for flavour or looks. Grow all three.

For spring harvesting: 'Hispi' – a delicious and quick to mature green cabbage.

How to grow

Start cabbages off under cover in modules or guttering: in March/April for summer- and autumn-hearting varieties; April/May for winter-hearting ones; and in July and August for spring-maturing types. Plant them out around 6 weeks after sowing, when 7 or 8cm tall, at the distance recommended on the seed packet (usually 25cm for smaller varieties, and twice that for larger ones). Water them in well, and tread around them to firm the ground.

Don't let them dry out, as you're after good steady growth. You'll find little else to do in the way of maintenance, apart from picking off the odd caterpillar.

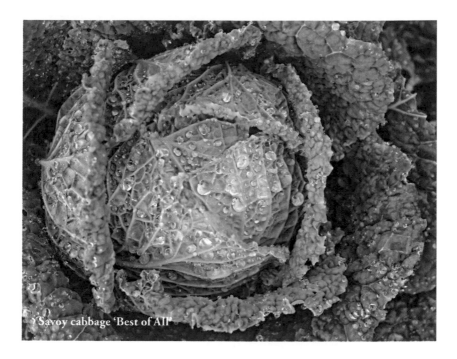
Savoy cabbage 'Best of All'

How to harvest

Timing will depend on your choice of varieties, but you will easily recognise the moment when the centre forms a relatively solid heart – use secateurs or a fairly solid knife to cut the head free. I don't let all of my cabbages mature. Instead I take a cut-and-come-again approach to them, diving in early to harvest odd leaves from at least half of the plants, and leaving the rest to form hearts for harvesting later.

Problems and pests

Caterpillars can decimate your cabbages, so either net plants through the growing season, or pick the pests off regularly and squash any eggs you come across. They seem less attracted to red varieties, so there's another reason to grow some. Slugs can be a problem even to established plants, so keep checking for them.

How to eat

Some cabbages, including Savoy, are wonderful raw, or sliced thinly and sautéed in olive oil, with tomatoes and herbs. Cabbage (and other brassicas) makes a tasty pasta sauce. Steam leaves until tender, then chop finely and throw into a pan for a few minutes with a little oil and garlic. Toss with the pasta and a touch of cream. Add chilli, herbs, Parmesan, etc, as you prefer. For more recipes, see pp.223, 255.

Calabrese *Brassica oleracea* var. *italica*

PLANT GROUP	Brassicas (see p.159)
START UNDER COVER	March–May
PLANT OUT	April–June
SOW DIRECT	March–May
HARVEST	June–September

This is the ever-popular vegetable most of us call broccoli. I must confess that although I like calabrese my heart really lies with sprouting broccoli, so I don't give these plants the space others might do. More recently, they've started to creep over a bit more of the plot, as my 3-year-old daughter loves eating their florets snapped straight from the plant. And if you're trying to grow your own and have young children, you'll know that anything which can keep them happily occupied for a few precious moments (while you do something they construe as 'dull') is gold.

Varieties
'Crown and Sceptre' and 'Chevalier' (F1) are top varieties for taste and reliability.

How to grow
Start them off under cover in modules or Jiffy 7s (see p.197) in early March, or sow the seed straight into your plot a couple of weeks later. Final spacing should be at least 30cm between plants. Spread your sowings by a fortnight to give a steady supply over a couple of months. If you are especially keen on calabrese, you can grow the plants in the ground in a polytunnel or greenhouse, sowing as late as early October for an early spring crop.

Calabrese is fairly low maintenance once established, but do keep your plants from drying out. It is steady, unchecked growth that you are looking for, after all.

How to harvest
You should get a harvest around 3–4 months after sowing, depending on the variety you are growing and the weather. Cut the heads from the plant with a good bit of stalk, and you should get side florets following on.

Problems and pests
Calabrese can provide hostelling facilities to any number of caterpillars, so look out for them and pick them off the plants as you spot them. And do soak the heads well in salty water before cooking to procure any that have kept hidden. Good job my daughter can't read that last bit.

How to eat

Calabrese takes very well to the pasta sauce treatment suggested for cabbages (see p.45). It also makes an excellent addition to your veg tempura (see p.233). If you are serving calabrese as a side veg, first steam it and then give it a good dressing. This can be as simple as good olive oil, black pepper and sea salt, or a classic vinaigrette. Or try this favourite dressing: mix a little finely chopped parsley with ½ tsp wholegrain mustard, a chopped garlic glove, ½ finely chopped red chilli, a pinch of sea salt and 100ml natural yoghurt. Pour over the hot calabrese and serve.

For more recipes, see pp.244, 250, 251.

Calabrese 'Chevalier'

Cardoons *Cynara cardunculus*

PLANT GROUP	Perennials (see p.169)
START UNDER COVER	March–April
PLANT OUT	May–June
HARVEST	October–November

Belonging to the thistle family, the cardoon looks a little as you might imagine a thistly celery on steroids. It is easily mistaken for the globe artichoke, whose flavour it somewhat resembles, but don't be tempted to investigate the flowerheads. It is the deliciously succulent inner stems and heart that you are after.

Many believe that to enjoy cardoons at their best you need to exclude the light, by binding the leaves tightly to the plant (a process known as 'blanching'). But even if you don't make time for blanching, the young stems are a truly delicious autumnal treat. If all you grow them for is their beauty and insect-attracting flowers, they are well worth the little effort required.

Varieties
Cardoons are often sold as an unnamed variety, but if you can source it, try 'Gigante di Romagna' as it is large and deliciously reliable.

How to grow
I sow them under cover in Jiffy 7s (see p.197) or pots in early spring, getting them out in the plot as soon as they are several centimetres tall. Planting at least 80cm apart should give them plenty of room to develop. Add compost or manure to the soil to get them growing quickly.

If you have planted cardoons in a windy site, stake them well as they grow. In autumn, when the flowers and long stems dry out, chop them back hard to encourage fresh growth.

How to harvest
Cardoons will quickly make a good height to add structure to your veg plot, and by late summer you can always tie up the stems and leaves to blanch the tender hearts for eating – a process that takes around 6 weeks. The stalks quickly flop when cut, so be sure to harvest them when you're ready to cook.

Problems and pests
You'll need to avoid slugs during the first weeks after planting out, but thereafter pests shouldn't be a problem.

Cardoon flowerheads

How to eat

Whether or not your cardoons are blanched, you will need to snip out the leafy part from the midrib. For the simplest cooking treatment, braise or steam the stalks for around half an hour until tender. They will be gorgeous with any of the sauces that suit globe artichokes, or you could try serving them with a mustardy/garlicky/anchovy mayonnaise.

Cardoon stalks are also worth the trouble of breadcrumbing and frying. Use a peeler to strip off the tough outer strings from half a kilo of stalks and chop them into 5cm lengths, popping them into a bowl of water acidulated with some lemon juice or white wine vinegar as you go. Boil for half an hour, then drain, dry and let them cool. Beat 2 egg yolks and 1 whole egg together. In another bowl, mix a handful of breadcrumbs with as much Parmesan and salt and pepper as you like. Heat a shallow layer of vegetable oil in a large frying pan until fairly hot. Dip the chopped stalks in the egg mix, then into the crumbs to coat, then add them to the pan. Fry until crisp and golden, drain on a wire rack and sprinkle with salt. Serve hot, with lemon wedges and mayonnaise.

Carrots *Daucus carota*

PLANT GROUP	Roots (see p.162)
SOW DIRECT	March–June
HARVEST	May–November

Recently I've come to see carrots in a new light. I now think of them as two very distinct vegetables: summer carrots and winter carrots, and use them accordingly. Think 'S' for summer carrots – small, sweet, salad, stir-fry, six-minutes' steaming. Winter carrots can be equally, if differently, delicious – roast them slowly with robust flavours, such as garlic and rosemary. Carrots also have an affinity with the seeds from most of their Umbelliferae cousins, including cumin, parsley, dill and fennel, although the judicious cook may want to steer clear of hemlock recipes.

The first time I grew carrots I set up an elaborate fence around them: rabbits eat carrots, everybody knows. The rabbits came and munched the brassicas to pieces. The fence blew over, but it made no difference – the rabbits tore through the cabbages. I've still never seen a rabbit eat a carrot... apart from Bugs Bunny. I've since discovered that his casual carrot-crunching wasn't anything to do with our toothy friends favouring them out in the field. Rather it came about from Clark Gable eating carrots while nonchalantly leaning against a fence talking to Claudette Colbert in the movie *It Happened One Night*. So now I know who to blame...

Varieties

Spring-sown 'Nantes' and 'Chantenay' give speedy returns in summer; summer-sown 'Autumn King' is good for harvesting from late autumn onwards. If your soil is on the heavier side, try the spring-sown 'Parabell', a small, almost-spherical carrot, best eaten at squash-ball size.

Carrots were originally purple, and can also be grown in red, white or yellow varieties. Resist the temptation to grow these novelties – almost without exception, they are as tasty as a trowel.

Choice of variety is particularly important, but to get the maximum taste out of your harvest it's worth going to the trouble of planting a few complimentary herbs, such as coriander and rosemary.

How to grow

Carrots are best sown direct. The lighter the soil the better, but carrots will do fine in whatever your soil type if you take time to prepare a good deep tilth. Pick a site with few stones, and don't be tempted to add manure to the ground, unless (like me) you find eternal amusement in forked carrots.

Early summer carrots lifted in May

Rake and water the bed well, and sow your seeds direct from March through to June. Sow seed every 30cm for larger winter roots, or as I prefer, mix the seed with a little sand and sow thinly, to give bunches of smaller carrots in the warm months. Cover the seed with a thin layer of compost. Sow summer carrots successively (small sowings, every few weeks) for a steady supply rather than a glut. Whatever size you're after, try to sow as close to the final spacing as you need, as thinning releases volatile chemicals that attract carrot flies.

Little ongoing care is required, other than ensuring that your carrots don't dry out and that they are well weeded.

How to harvest

Pull summer carrots as soon as they are ready (from May onwards), leaving any smaller ones in the ground to develop a little. Winter carrots are usually fine left in the ground until you're ready to eat them. However, if you know you're approaching a really rainy period, pull to prevent them sending out extra fine roots. If you're lifting them well before eating, store them unwashed in a wine crate (or similar) full of slightly damp sand, or in paper sacks that exclude the light.

Problems and pests

Carrot fly is the pest you will need to guard against. Comfrey or seaweed solution (see p.215) helps to discourage the fly as well as encourage the plant. Companion planting from the strong-smelling onion family (try chives or spring onions) works pretty well as the fly navigates by smell. That said, a protection of horticultural fleece is an accessory often worn in the second year as a lesson learned from the first.

How to eat

Eat carrots straight from the ground especially during the summer, brushing off the soil with your hands. Or steam them for a few minutes until tender but retaining a bite and serve with a light dressing or good butter. Juice winter carrots with apples for a beautifully tasty vitamin boost, or roast them with honey (see p.253). Carrots also make a wonderful soup, especially with the addition of coriander and/or parsley, and no stock is complete without them (see p.259). For more recipes, see pp.223, 225, 233, 250, 260.

Cauliflowers *Brassica oleracea* var. *botrytis*

PLANT GROUP	Brassicas (see p.159)
START UNDER COVER	Summer cauliflowers: January–March; Winter cauliflowers: April–July
PLANT OUT	Summer cauliflowers: March–May; Winter cauliflowers: July–October
HARVEST	All year, depending on sowing time:– Summer cauliflowers: June–October Winter cauliflowers: November–May

This is one of those vegetables that few dislike but fewer really love. I suspect it's because few of us have enjoyed them at their best. They may never be the most flavourful feast from your plot, but grow your own and you'll be bowled over by their stunning smell alone.

I certainly didn't like cauliflower when I was young. I'd seen a brain on TV when I was tucking into cauliflower cheese as a child and a switch was clicked. Fortunately, a few years ago, my favourite Indian takeaway reaquainted me with the delights of this vegetable and I now find cauliflowers creeping across the plot in ever-increasing numbers.

You can grow cauliflowers all year round, but I'd urge you to grow them through the winter when they are easy and productive, serving up tasty heads during the leaner months into early spring. Cauliflowers grown through the summer are high maintenance, needing endless watering and feeding if you're to get perfect white globes to harvest. It's not to say that they are impossible, but you'll need to be a real devotee and prepared to commit the time, the care, and a little love to get what you're after. I prefer it slightly easier – I'm busy enough in the summer with all the others in the veg patch to be over-attending a 'special' one.

Varieties

With a spread of varieties you can have delicious cauliflowers all year round. Unsurprisingly, 'All Year Round' does what it says, producing good-sized white cauliflowers whenever you want them, although most people sow from early spring until June for a late summer through autumn crop. I prefer to go for some of the winter varieties such as 'Purple Cape' that are ready in March to May when there's not a whole lot about.

The conical 'Romanesco' variety, with its incredible fractal, self-replicating pattern is as impressive on the plate as it is in your plot. It is also sold by some as a variety of calabrese.

Cauliflower 'Romanesco'

How to grow

This is the ultimate seed packet veg: check the sowing times and stick to them. If you sow them any earlier, your cauliflowers will probably bolt on you. I sow all mine under cover, in modules, planting them out when they are around 7–10cm tall. Steady growth is what you're after, so give them a sheltered site in full sun, prepare the bed well in autumn with compost, plant them out 65cm apart and tread the soil down well to anchor the shallow-rooting plants.

If you want to produce really beautiful cauliflowers, then it's worth the trouble of bending a few of the outer leaves over the developing curd to protect it – part snapping the central rib of the leaves helps keep them in place.

How to harvest

Cut off the globe when it has formed a dense hemisphere, before it gets a chance to bolt. You will need to keep a keen eye on them as this can happen almost overnight if the weather's hot.

Problems and pests

Cauliflower seedlings can be troubled by slugs and caterpillars, so pick off any you find. Once you've got your plants past the seedling stage, your troubles should be behind you.

Bolting – where the cauliflower bursts its globe skywards in little florets – is your main headache if you're growing cauliflower in summer. In warm sun, they grow rapidly, forming heads very easily and are liable to run to seed. Although bolting tends to be caused by the extra light and heat that comes with long summer days, watering seems to arrest this urge, so get ready with the watering can if you've not had much rain.

How to eat

The complex, subtle taste of cauliflower is wonderful either raw or cooked laden with spices – somehow it survives even a fairly robust heat treatment. If you break or cut your cauliflower into florets, steaming takes only 10 minutes or so. If you're in any doubt, err slightly on the underdone side – the last thing you want to do is overcook it. Rarely has a home-grown vegetable shown the importance of fine texture better than the cauliflower.

Another lovely way of serving cauliflower is to cook and serve it whole, smothered in a dressing made from ½ finely chopped garlic clove, 6 chopped anchovies, 50ml lemon juice and a pinch of cayenne pepper, whisked together with 100ml olive oil.

For more recipes, see pp.223, 233.

Celeriac *Apium graveolens* var. *rapaceum*

PLANT GROUP	Roots (see p.162)
START UNDER COVER	February–March
PLANT OUT	May–June
HARVEST	September–March

Not someone addicted to celery, but a root of the same family with a comparable, yet sweeter, slightly peppery, nutty flavour. Shop-bought, you'll get a knobbly fighter's fist of a root, but home-grown celeriac has the added bonus of a crown of celery-like stalks – great chopped finely into soup bases. Celeriac has the ability to absorb flavours without losing itself and it works well with many partners, not least cream. Distinctive and versatile, it features in many culinary classics.

Varieties
'Prinz' is the most widely available variety and rarely disappoints.

How to grow
You can sow celeriac direct, but you'll risk slugs and snails attacking the emerging seedlings. I sow mine under cover in February–March in modules. Hardening off for a week or so works really well with celeriac, resulting in fewer failures and reducing the number that go to seed. Plant them out in May, 40cm apart. Celeriac will tolerate light shade, but the soil should be kept moist in dry weather.

How to harvest
Although celeriac can take over 4 months to reach maturity, it will keep in the ground until March. After harvesting, store with the leaves removed for longevity.

Problems and pests
Other than slugs attacking emerging seedlings, you're unlikely to suffer any other nuisances. Celery fly maggots might (if you're very unlucky) damage plants in early spring. To avoid this, you can plant seedlings out a little later, from May onwards.

How to eat
Peel celeriac and drop into water acidulated with lemon juice to prevent discolouring. Blanching celeriac in boiling water for 1 minute then refreshing in cold water takes the edge off any bitterness – worth doing if you're using it raw in salad. Try layering slices alternately with potato for a lovely variation of dauphinoise (see p.254); or in a half-and-half mix for mash. For more recipes, see pp.225, 227, 228, 250.

Celeriac 'Prinz'

Celery *Apium graveolens* var. *dulce*

PLANT GROUP	Roots (see p.162)
START UNDER COVER	February–March
PLANT OUT	May–June
HARVEST	August–October

As their names suggest, celery and celeriac are closely related. Even if you're not one of those who love the unusual tang of raw celery, grow it for its marvellous ability to bring out the best in others, notably in stocks, stews and soups.

Varieties

Older varieties are grown in trenches, gradually earthed up as they grow. Happily, new self-blanching varieties avoid this palaver. 'Golden Self Blanching', 'Daybreak' and 'Green Utah' are all excellent varieties that need no blanching (see p.18).

How to grow

Sow seed under cover in early spring in modules or Jiffy 7s (see p.197), shifting them into pots, 7.5cm across. Harden off for a few days when the first proper leaves have formed in May or June, before planting out 25cm apart. Celery likes a moisture-retentive, well-drained soil in a sunny spot – add compost and/or well-rotted manure a few months before if you can. Keep celery from drying out, and keep it well weeded until the plants are large enough to shade out any competing weeds.

How to harvest

Harvest self-blanching varieties before the frosts, when the sticks are recognisable in their usual form, from around August to October.

Problems and pests

Starting celery off under cover minimises slug and snail damage. Planting out from May onwards avoids celery fly maggots (which tend to trouble celery in April).

How to eat

In my view, celery works best in combination with garlic, onions and carrots, as the underpinning base of any number of stocks and stews. If you're looking for it to take centre stage, then try serving it as a gratin: boil in salted water for 10 minutes, drain and lay in a buttered ovenproof dish, then just cover with béchamel sauce, dot with a few knobs of butter and grate over lots of Parmesan. Bake at 190°C/Gas Mark 5 for 15 minutes or until golden. For more recipes, see pp.228, 256, 259.

Celery 'Green Utah'

Chard _Beta vulgaris_ var. _flavescens_
and Perpetual Spinach _Beta vulgaris_ var. _cicla_

PLANT GROUP	Others (see p.169)
START UNDER COVER	March–August
PLANT OUT	April–October
SOW DIRECT	April–August
HARVEST	All year

As their Latin name attests, chard and perpetual spinach are almost one and the same, each giving you delicious year-round leaves for the minimum of trouble. I have a few chard plants that are still throwing out tasty leaves 17 months after sowing, somehow avoiding the attention of the slugs, snails and caterpillars. Many growers undervalue those plants that almost seem to cut themselves and hop into your basket, but don't take offence at their lack of reliance on you – love them all the more for their quiet self-sufficiency.

Beyond being easy as it gets to grow, they'll do much to liven up the look of your patch. Green-and-white Swiss chard was made for the frosts to dust with ice crystals, and the richly coloured varieties add a vibrant flourish to any plot.

Varieties
Swiss chard and perpetual spinach are often sold as unnamed generic seed, but it's worth searching out 'White Silver' for its delicious green-and-white leaves. Colourful rhubarb and rainbow chard make tasty additions to the plot – 'Bright Lights' is the variety I grow every year. Most varieties picked small will give you tender salad leaves, but 'Canary Yellow' chard (with its yellow ribs) is perhaps the best. 'Popeye' is, appropriately, the best named variety of perpetual spinach.

How to grow
Success with either chard or perpetual spinach is pretty well assured. Germination rates are high, and so good is their ability to regrow, you'll only need two sowings to get cut-and-come-again leaves all year. Your first sowing should be in March. Sow under cover in Jiffy 7s (see p.197) or modules and plant out 6 weeks later at least 50cm apart, or sow direct in April. Your second sowing, for winter and early spring eating, should be in August, direct or under cover. Don't get anxious if your sowings take a little while to appear – a few weeks for any sign of growth is normal.

Apart from giving them a little water in a drought, chard and perpetual spinach need no routine care other than weeding.

How to harvest

You'll be harvesting your first cut of leaves around 10 weeks after sowing – either cut leaves or tear them off from the outside of the plant or chop the whole lot a few centimetres above ground level, and new leaves will grow in their place.

Problems and pests

Slugs and snails may trouble young seedlings. Starting them off under cover helps get the plant to a size that limits the extent of the damage, but keep an eye out.

How to eat

Strip the stems from the leaves and steam them for 3–4 minutes before adding the torn-off leaves for another 2 minutes. As a side vegetable, olive oil and salt is all that is needed, although a little chopped chilli won't go amiss. Both chard and perpetual spinach are lovely chopped and cooked with Puy lentils, and work well as the leaves in half the garden soup (see p.223). For more recipes, see pp.244, 248.

Chard 'Bright Lights'

Chicory *Cichorium intybus*

PLANT GROUP	Salad leaves (see p.166)
SOW DIRECT	May–July
HARVEST	October–January

I grew chicory for the first time only a couple of years ago and it won me over immediately, although the bitterness can be an acquired taste for some. You can grow chicory either for salad leaves or for hearts, which are usually cooked. Think of chicory and endive (see p.74) as the 'olives' of the salad bowl. The first taste of each may leave you uncertain, but once it's clicked with you – and it will – you'll not want to be without them.

Bear in mind that chicory hearts tend to be sweeter than the individual leaves, so it's worth growing some for leaves and others for hearts, giving you two very different leafy flavours from just one sowing. Added to that, chicory looks good, grows well in the darker months and delivers in the leaner weeks.

Varieties
The hardy 'Rossa di Treviso' (also known as 'Treviso Rosso'), one of the radicchio types of chicory, has been the taste and visual success of all the chicories I've tried – both for its hearts and its reddy-purple/acid-green leaves. 'Palla Rossa' is similarly beautiful, easy to grow, very hardy, and forms delicious dense heads. 'Sugar Loaf', with its crisp green hearts and leaves, is wonderfully tasty, and has a good resistance to bolting even when grown in a polytunnel. 'Variegata di Castelfranco' is an excellent traditional variety that I have found to be happily reliable for either cut-and-come-again leaves or for allowing to heart up.

How to grow
Sow direct in late spring and early summer, thinning the plants to 5cm apart for small leaves, 25cm for larger leaves or hearts, in rows around 25cm apart.

How to harvest
Chicory is one of those delightfully useful harvests that not only endures the cold, it positively thrives in it. With good care, regular picking, and a little bit of luck, you can expect leaves and hearts right through the coldest months of the year, with cut-and-come-agains staying slowly productive for up to 4 months. Once you've had some success with chicories and taken them to heart, investigate a few more varieties. There's an amazing range of textures and tastes out there – check the catalogues and seed packets.

You can force chicory, but lovely as it may be, it has always seemed one step too far for me, involving digging up and so forth, so I've never bothered.

Problems and pests

Rather in the way we don't tend to do 'bitter' flavours very much in this country, few pests do either, which is fortunate.

How to eat

A few leaves work well in a salad, where chicory's slight bitterness will offset a range of milder wintery leaves beautifully. Chicory is also delicious braised, and works well in risottos.

If you're looking for it to take centre stage, quarter 3 chicory heads and blanch them in water acidulated with lemon juice for a couple of minutes. Drain thoroughly and allow them to cool. Crumble 100g blue cheese into a small pan, add 80ml double cream and warm through until the cheese just starts to melt. Take off the heat and season with freshly ground black pepper (the cheese will add the saltiness). Heat 20g butter in a frying pan and add the chicory, cooking it until it starts to colour. Serve the chicory warm, dressed with the blue cheese dressing and scattered with a few crushed toasted walnuts. For more recipes, see pp. 248, 250.

Chicory 'Rossa di Treviso'

Picking chillies 'Cayenne Long Slim'

Chilli peppers *Capsicum annuum*

PLANT GROUP	Solanaceae (see p.168)
START UNDER COVER	February–April
PLANT OUT	June
HARVEST	August–October

Chilli peppers are one of the most potent of 'transformers', lending a gastronomic hand to so many of your other harvests. All that flavour from such a little pod makes them a real must, whether you've a rural smallholding or an urban window ledge. Everything from potatoes to salads is lifted by the spicy punch of chilli, and with careful selection of variety to suit your preference for heat, you'll find them a hugely rewarding harvest.

If you do not have a polytunnel or greenhouse, pop your chilli plants on your sunniest windowsill. Many varieties love the restricted root run they get in a pot, and in your home they'll benefit from you being able to keep a close eye on them as they develop. Once under way, chilli plants grow quickly from tiny seedlings into beautiful (almost Christmassy) bushes. Even on a windowsill, don't be surprised to get a couple of dozen chillies or more from each one.

Varieties

'Hungarian Hot Wax' is a favourite, producing its long and pointed fruit over a relatively short season. This gives them a racing chance of maturing even in a disappointing summer. Not only that, their heat alters with its colour – pick them green and mild, through yellow to fiery red. 'Jalapeño' is similarly excellent.

If you are looking for the best variety for indoor pot growing, go for 'Apache', which is a smaller variety and pretty much in the centre of the heat spectrum. 'Poblano' is hard to beat for times when you're after something on the milder side of hot and is ideal for stuffings or salsas. If you can handle it, try any of the ridiculously hot Habanero varieties – keep some yoghurt handy as it alleviates the burning sensation (from your mouth at least).

How to grow

I sow mine under cover in March in Jiffy 7s (see p.197) or small pots and keep them either at bench height or on a windowsill in the house for the extra warmth – chillies hate the cold and the wet. Don't start them off after April – they are sun lovers and need a long season to make it to their best. Peppers are slow to germinate, taking up to a month, so try popping them in the airing cupboard to speed things up – by as much as two-thirds. Make sure, however, that you take them out as soon as they poke out of the compost. Pot them into 9cm pots and on to larger ones as soon as the roots start to poke out. Get them into the ground (ideally under cover) or into their final pot in June.

Chillies are less trouble to the grower than tomatoes, but less reliable in coming to full ripeness. Comfrey waterings (see p.215) or sprays given from flowering onwards will nudge you ever nearer to a top crop, but don't overwater them, and do tie the plants to a stake for support. It is also a good idea to limit the height (essential if you're growing them in pots), so pinch out the growing tips to encourage them to bush out.

How to harvest

Pick and use them fresh at their peak – usually September or so, depending on how sunny the summer has been. Then, as the sunlight hours fall in mid-autumn, pick any that remain and dry them in an oven on its lowest setting overnight for use over the following months.

Problems and pests

You'll rarely find your chilli plants troubled. If you do, it will probably be aphids (see pp.217–18 for remedies).

How to eat

Chilli adds heat and colour to a host of dishes. Use it where you like, but be adventurous as it works surprisingly well with many less obvious partners. The confit chilli (see p.230) will go with just about anything.

For a deliciously different take on scrambled eggs: add ½ finely chopped onion and ½ finely chopped garlic clove to a drop of olive oil in a hot pan. Cook for a few minutes, then add a couple of peeled, chopped tomatoes, a few chopped oregano leaves (go easy on these) and ½ finely chopped medium-hot chilli. In a bowl, beat 6 eggs lightly and add them to the pan, mixing everything together well with a wooden spoon. Push the eggs around the pan with the spoon and, just as they begin to scramble, throw in a few pitted olives. Serve with toast.

For more recipes, see pp.242, 256, 259.

Courgettes *Cucurbita pepa*

PLANT GROUP	Cucurbits (see p.165)
START UNDER COVER	April–June
PLANT OUT	May–July
HARVEST	July–October

An ideal plant for the beginner or the nervous grower – once planted out, you can almost ignore courgettes. They really do grow quickly, easily and abundantly to the point where they are almost reviled for their productivity. This is one harvest you needn't worry about maximising. The secret of enjoying it to the full is to grow only a few plants, harvest them as tasty cigars, and have a few belting recipes up your sleeve for the excess that's coming your way.

Growing courgettes also lets you in on one of those unique home-grown harvests – their flowers. These store and travel poorly, so growing your own is the only way to lay your hands on them at their peak. They are truly delicious, with a distinctive sweet, mildly peppery flavour that almost feels like you are tasting the pollen.

Varieties
Try 'Arbarello di Sarzarno' or 'Soleil' (F1) for delicious, long cigars; 'Rondo di Nizza' for wonderful green globes, ideal for stuffing; and 'Trombomcino' as a tasty climber ideal for tepeeing in pots.

How to grow
Start courgettes off under cover in small pots in April, hardening them off for a couple of days before planting them out about 60cm apart when you're confident you've seen the last frost. Two sowings – one in early spring, one in early summer – should keep you in fruit right into autumn.

Make sure they have plenty of water during the first weeks after planting out. Also water the plants through dry periods, though you'll probably find that their leaves help to retain soil moisture, and handily suppress weeds. A fortnightly comfrey feed (see p.215) from flowering onwards will give them a boost if you're after maximum yield, though you should find them perfectly productive without.

How to harvest
In truth, it's pretty hard to go wrong with courgettes – all you have to do is avoid leaving them to get too large. If you do, flavourless exhibition fruit will result and the plant will stop producing those sweet cigars that should be your aim. The only rule is 'keep picking'.

Problems and pests

Starting courgettes off under cover ensures that they get to a good size before arriving in your veg patch, by which stage slug and snail damage will usually be minimal. There are a range of viruses and mildews that may affect your courgette plants. For the most part you will still get a crop, but you'll need to remove any badly affected plants and burn them.

How to eat

Delicious though ratatouille can be, maximising the versatility of courgettes will help you make the best of what will be plentiful. Try them grated raw in salads, or dress thin slices with oil and lemon, salt and pepper and any of the annual herbs. Chilli and pine nuts will happily sit by their side, and they make a perfect partner for Parmesan. Courgettes are also the ideal barbecue veg, taking to the griddle almost as well as a steak.

Torn into salads, the flowers make a vibrant addition, but are perhaps best as a wonderful cup for stuffing and deep-frying (see p.234). Go for the male flowers, as they have no young courgette developing behind them.

For more recipes, see pp.223, 237, 248, 256.

Courgettes 'Arbarello di Sarzarno'

Cucumbers and Gherkins
Cucumis sativus

PLANT GROUP	Cucurbits (see p.165)
START UNDER COVER	March–May
PLANT OUT	May–June
HARVEST	July–October

If you want to see the importance of texture to culinary pleasure and just what a difference it can make to the very best ingredients, grow your own cucumbers and gherkins. They may not be at the top of the in-your-face flavour bombs that the gardener can grow, but try 'Crystal Lemon' cucumbers and 'Vert Petit de Paris' gherkins and I'm sure you'll find them a revelation of cool crunch. I'd no sooner be without my own than I would salad leaves.

Added to that, the plants look beautiful and could be grown by the most inexperienced gardener, so find room for even just a couple of plants. Sea salt, freshly ground pepper, olive oil – and a hot day on which to appreciate their coolness – are all the accompaniments they need.

Varieties
'Crystal Lemon' is outstanding, giving you cool, yellow globes of summer freshness. 'Marketmore' is a great all-rounder, suitable for indoors and out. Some cucumber seed is sold as an outdoor variety (check the catalogue or seed packet). If you're growing these then leave all flowers on, but don't grow more than one variety as they may cross-pollinate, leading to bitterness in the fruit.

'Eureka' (F1) and 'Vert Petit de Paris' are wonderfully delicious and reliable gherkin varieties that grow really well outside, either over a structure or allowed to scramble over the ground.

How to grow
Jiffy 7s (see p.197) and small pots are best for starting off cucumbers and gherkins. I get them going under cover in March or April, potting them on as needed until planting out in May (after hardening off for a couple of days). Choose a sunny, sheltered site, and leave a good half-metre between plants. Some varieties will do well outside in a good summer but all will be more reliable under cover, cropping earlier and for longer. Cucumbers and gherkins like to climb and scramble, and although you won't need to support the fruits themselves, canes give the plant a good structure to wind around.

The plants will need watering most days if grown under cover, and through any dry periods if they are outside. Increase watering as they grow. As with other cucurbits, comfrey feeds (see p.215) every fortnight after flowering starts will really give the plants – and hence your crops – a boost. Pinching out the shoot and growing tips helps focus the plant's energies on fruit production, but once in a while I haven't got round to it and I've still had excellent yields.

If you are growing cucumbers under cover, do check whether your chosen varieties are all female (many modern F1 cultivar are) or look for emerging male flowers. These have no small cucumber behind them in the way that female flowers do. You'll need to remove male flowers as they appear, because if female flowers are pollinated their fruit (and its eater) will turn bitter.

How to harvest

If you sow in April you can expect a good harvest from August onwards, although you can always try a March and May sowing too if you are particularly keen to maximise your chances of a long and heavy haul. Most varieties, especially 'Crystal Lemon', will be at their best if you pick them before they get too large and firm, before the skin thickens too much. Judging the best size is largely a matter of experimentation. Peel them if you leave it late and they'll still be delicious.

Problems and pests

Starting your plants off under cover minimises the chances of slug damage while the seedlings are small and vulnerable. After that, they should remain relatively untroubled. Cucumbers can be susceptible to mildew. Comfrey or seaweed solutions (see p.215) sprayed on the plants help to lessen the risk, but 'Burpless Tasty Green' (F1) is resistant to mildew, so growing a few of this variety ensures you'll have a cucumber crop even if the others succumb.

How to eat

Cucumber is a refreshing, cool addition to many summer salads, none finer than the classic Greek salad: put a thinly sliced cucumber into a large salad bowl with 4 large, juicy tomatoes, cored and cut into wedges. Crumble in 250g feta cheese (or similar crumbly, salty cheese) and add a couple of handfuls of pitted black olives. Drizzle over 90ml good olive oil and 30ml lemon juice, and season with freshly ground black pepper to taste. Mix very gently and sprinkle with a few torn basil or oregano leaves to serve.

For a sweet-sour treatment, marinate 2 peeled and thinly sliced cucumbers in a mixture of 50ml olive oil, 25ml white wine vinegar, 2 tbsp caster sugar, a small handful of finely chopped dill and plenty of salt and pepper to taste for an hour.

For more recipes, see pp.250, 251.

Cucumber 'Marketmore'

Edible flowers

I'm sure the idea of eating flowers won't appeal to some macho allotmenters, but the chances are they are eating some already... blissfully unaware. Cauliflower, broccoli, calabrese and artichokes are just a few of the flowers that most of us put away quite happily in their semi-mature state, but somehow it seems altogether weirder to give 'proper' flowers like nasturtiums a whirl.

I have to take my hat off to Sarah Raven who inspired me to try edible flowers. If you sit, as I did, grim-faced at the prospect, then I'd like to suggest courgette flowers as the best bridge for crossing the divide. It looks like a flower, it is a flower, but you can take comfort that at least it comes from a vegetable. Try them deep-fried (see p.234) and marvel at their pepperiness.

Most edible flowers won't give you any trouble, nor call on your time. Sow direct or in pots, at spacings advised on the packet. Don't let them dry out, and if you're growing them in pots most will welcome the odd comfrey feed (see p.215). Snip off unblemished flowers at their peak for eating, and tatty ones for the compost heap. This ensures the plant will keep producing new flowers over the following weeks.

Top flowers for the kitchen

In addition to my favourite courgette flowers (see p.67), try growing the following:

Borage This is the beautiful bee-attracting flower that adds colour to a jug of Pimms, along with leaves that bring a wonderful cucumber coolness to salads. Buy one packet and sow in spring. Borage's ability to self-seed ensures that you'll then have it for life. Freeze the flowers in ice cubes to drag your harvest into the winter.

Nasturtiums Happy in poor soil, nasturtium flowers taste almost as good as they look, bringing their sweet pepperiness to any summer salad. They are also perfect in tempura (see p.233). Sow them in spring, either in lines (5–10cm apart) or just broadcast in a patch and thin if you think they're getting too cramped. Some, like 'Black Velvet', will climb if you give them structure, or creep over the ground if you don't. 'Tip Top Mahogany' is probably the pick of the bunch – its peppery leaves are the strongest of the ones I've grown. Even the seed pods are edible – and, if you eat a couple of dozen at the first inkling, reputedly ward off colds.

Viola Start them off in spring under cover and the pansy-like flowers will bring a colourful, sweet and fragrant twist to mid-summer, autumn and winter salads without having the peppery hit of many of the other edible flowers.

Calendula (pot marigold) Sprinkled over salads, the petals add a bright-orange dash, and if you're after something different try using them with rice, where they bring a colour and taste close to saffron but for a fraction of the price. Not to be confused with marigold (*Tagetes* sp.), which is a fine companion plant (see p.212).

Herb flowers The flowers of most herbs are also edible; some – like chive flowers – are particularly delicious. As a rule of thumb, you'll find they taste very much like the more-used parts (if perhaps slightly stronger or milder). Fennel, dill, thyme and oregano flowers are all worth trying, allowing you to add their familiar flavour to your food in a beautifully different way.

Borage

Endive *Cichorium endivia*

PLANT GROUP	Salad leaves (see p.166)
SOW DIRECT	May–August
HARVEST	August–March

With its tasty bitterness, endive – like chicory – adds to your cooking options over the colder half of the year. As with chicory, you have the choice of growing it for leaves or hearts, although endive plants are altogether more floppy and informal. I love endive, though not in large quantities, so I grow only a few plants and I suggest you do the same if you're new to them.

If you are not convinced by the bitterness of this salad veg, you can always take the edge off it with a little simple blanching. When your endive resemble upturned mop heads, place a large pot over a couple of them (with the holes blocked to exclude all light). Uncover them after 3 weeks or so and they should be paler, sweeter, and delicious. Leave the unblanched endive to grow on slowly until you are ready to blanch a few more.

Varieties

'Fine de Louvier' is excellent for leaves, 'Blond Full Heart' for hearts, while 'Cuor d'Oro' is hard to beat for productivity and doesn't need blanching – it turns itself white. Consider 'Cornet de Bordeaux' if you want to grow endive through winter.

How to grow

Endive seeds are best thinly sown straight into your plot, thinning the plants as they grow to allow 25cm between plants. Sow from late spring until mid-summer, – exactly when will depend on the variety, so check the catalogue or seed packet. If you are growing endive for hearts, sow them successively in smaller batches to avoid them all maturing at the same time.

Endive plants are pretty low maintenance, although you may need to water them a little in a hot, dry patch to prevent bolting.

How to harvest

You can crop endive for a good 6 months or more from August onwards, which makes them a wonderfully enduring addition to your autumn and winter options. Endive is excellent for cut-and-come-again leaf harvesting, or if you have a hearting variety such as 'Blond Full Heart', you can let them develop until the hearts are saucer-sized and try the quick blanching technique. If you're harvesting the whole blanched head, slice it off at soil level using a long knife.

Problems and pests

Problems are rare. Slugs and snails are usually put off by endive's bitterness, but do check the plants occasionally, especially if you are blanching them under pots.

How to eat

If you are unsure about bitter leaves, try a few 'Fine de Louvier' endive as your way in. The cut leaves make a bright, edgy contrast scattered sparingly into a mixed leaf salad, or as a leafy salad on their own with a honey mustard dressing.

Surprisingly perhaps, endive is also delicious fried: blanch in boiling water for a couple of minutes, drain and dry well. Season generously, then fold the outer leaves around the paler centre to keep it crisp and succulent. Heat a little olive oil in a frying pan and fry the endive on one side until it starts to brown, then flip over to fry the other side. It's lovely eaten on its own, but particularly good with fish.

Or try sliced endive hearts fried in tempura batter (see p.233) – they're fantastic. For more recipes, see pp.226, 250.

Endive 'Cuor d'Oro'

Florence fennel

Foeniculum vulgare var. *azoricum*

PLANT GROUP	Others (see p.169)
SOW DIRECT	April–July
HARVEST	June–November

Closely related to the feathery fennel herb, grown predominantly for its leaves and seeds, Florence fennel varieties bulk up at the base into the classic aromatic bulbs. Their distinctive flavour comes from a compound also found in star anise, and I love the cool taste as much cooked as I do raw. Aniseed may not be everyone's glass of Pernod, but even if you are unsure it's really worth giving fennel's mild, sweet bulbs a try. As with celery, even if the naked veg isn't to your taste, it has the ability to make others shine a little brighter. Try the various different ways of serving it and let fennel work its magic throughout a meal.

Easy to grow and one of the most beautiful vegetables there is, fennel is worth its place in your patch for its striking presence alone.

Varieties
Reliable, delicious and tender, 'Romanesco' is a must. If you have trouble with fennel bolting, try 'Finale', which is slower to run to seed than other varieties.

How to grow
Sow direct from late April–May onwards for best results, thinning out the emerging seedlings to 25cm each way. If you're desperate for an early start, then you can sow varieties that resist bolting, such as 'Finale', as early as the end of February since they'll happily grow through the heat of high summer. You can leave some to produce into the colder months, cutting them back often to encourage more succulent growth. Fennel isn't fussy when it comes to soil. It will do well anywhere, but do give it some sun and regular (but not too much) water.

Problems and pests
Fennel is very rarely troubled by anything.

How to harvest
The bulbs will be ready from late July through to November (or from late June if you have sown early varieties). If you've sown a good number, you can start harvesting earlier when they're smaller.

While the bulbs are developing, pinch off some of the tendrilly top growth too – use it to add a clean aniseedy hit to salads and dressings. If you cut the bulbs about 3cm above ground, the remaining stump may well sprout again through the following months. Do leave some to grow on unharvested – they add decorative structure to the veg patch... and the insects will love you for it.

How to eat

Fennel has proven to be a real four-course favourite of mine, turning out refreshing cool soups, livening up salads, finding a heaven-made match with fish and cheese, and, as the Italians do, you can take it one course further and serve it with fruit.

It delivers not just in flavour, but equally importantly in its texture. Wonderfully crisp raw, firm to squidgy when roasted or boiled, fennel is a classic whatever-the-weather vegetable that is resilient enough to work just as well as leftovers the following day. It makes a perfect addition to the crudités list, a wonderful griddled partner to fish and chicken, and if the bulbs flower try the umbrella in tempura batter (see p.233). For more recipes, see pp.242, 244, 259.

Florence fennel 'Romanesco'

French beans 'Blauhilde'

French beans *Phaseolus vulgaris*

PLANT GROUP	Legumes (see p.157)
START UNDER COVER	March–July
PLANT OUT	May–August
SOW DIRECT	April–July
HARVEST	May–October

Smaller and rounder than runner beans, French beans come in climbing and dwarf varieties. Give both sorts a go, as there are some delicious varieties of each. They not only deliver in the kitchen, they'll add colour, variety and height to your plot too. Indeed many varieties were originally grown as ornamentals.

French beans are also just about as easy, productive and versatile as veg go. Not only do you get a great return from each plant, you have any number of opportunities to use the beans. Picked small they are delicious raw; left a little larger they are wonderful briefly steamed; once fully grown the beans can be podded and eaten in soups and stews, or saved for sowing the following year. A must for any plot.

Varieties

'Purple Teepee' (purple, dwarf), 'Blauhilde' (purple, climbing), 'Rocquencourt' (yellow, dwarf) and 'Blue Lake Climbing' (green, climbing) are all excellent.

How to grow

Bean seeds are pleasingly large for handling. It's worth soaking them for half an hour to soften their skin and encourage germination before you sow them. You can sow direct from mid-spring onwards, under cover from March for a June crop, and as late as July for an autumn haul. If you're starting them off indoors, try toilet roll inners or root trainers (see p.197) to allow their roots to develop a good run.

Don't be tempted to sow too many. Some varieties, including those above, are heavy croppers and you'll end up with a rather full chutney cupboard. Instead, sow three small batches 6 weeks apart for a steady supply. They'll germinate quickly in a bright, cool (but not cold) place. Let them get to a few centimetres tall before planting out, to increase their chances of dodging slugs.

The climbing varieties will need something to grow up or over. This can be anything from a few canes tied into rows or a tepee, to more elaborate arches and screens. If you're going for the tepee, ensure the pattern of canes in the ground is in a 'C' shape rather than a full circle so that you can get to the beans that grow towards the centre. If left unpicked, these will continue to develop far beyond the picking stage and take valuable resources from the plant, slowing production of the succulent beans you are after. If you are growing French beans in a line, give them a good 20cm between plants. Most beans love the sun, but watch the taller varieties for the wind. These energetic climbers can easily reach 2 metres, so pick a fairly sheltered spot... or don't, and watch them fall over as I did last year.

Beans love water from the stage when they are flowering, and watering with comfrey tea (see p.215) will promote healthy and extended production.

How to harvest

The main harvest is August and September, but if you're a fan you can stretch this from June through to November by sowing them successionally as recommended. Regular picking is essential, partly because the beans are at their best small, but also as it stimulates the plant to grow more and for longer. Try a few beans when they're small and smooth – they should snap easily in the middle when you bend them. It's worth using scissors or secateurs to harvest them as pulling often tears the plant itself. Once you can see the beans bulging in their pod they've got too large to be ideal, but still pick them to encourage more to grow, or if it is towards the end of the season let some fatten and the pods turn golden. Leave in place until the weather is about to turn wet, then cut the plant and hang it upside down somewhere light and airy until the pods really desiccate. Then shell the beans and allow them to dry for a few more days on paper. *Voilà*: haricot beans. Or next year's seed.

At the end of the season don't pull up the plants unless you've a crop going straight in. If you cut the plants clear, leaving the roots to breakdown into the soil, you'll be leaving a nutritious present for the next crop to enjoy (see p.157).

Problems and pests

Green and black aphids love beans almost as much as we do, so it's well worth planting a few flowers as companion plants in with the beans. Marigolds (*Tagetes* sp.) are particularly good at attracting the aphid-eating ladybirds and hoverflies. If you still get bothered, the best remedy is to rub or spray the aphids off with the hose. Slugs and snails can quickly decimate your crop – get in early and get in hard with as many remedies as you can manage (see p.216).

How to eat

Add beans to boiling salted water and cook until tender, but retaining a bite, then plunge briefly into ice-cold water to preserve colour, flavour and vigour. Most of those that are not already green, will be once cooked, but if you're after preserving a little of that garden colour try adding 1 tsp sugar to the cooking water.

French beans are fantastic with most of the dressings and sauces that work with asparagus, globe artichokes, sprouting broccoli and peas, but are perhaps best with a Japanese-style dressing (see p.251). For more recipes, see pp.223, 244, 256.

Garlic *Allium sativum*

PLANT GROUP	Onions (see p.164)
SOW DIRECT	October–November or February–March
HARVEST	May–September

I don't think there's another smell to match garlic for getting the gastronomic juices going. Chopped and thrown raw into salsa verde, or fried gently with onions, or roasted alongside tomatoes, the effect is the same – that aroma makes you hungry. And it's all thanks to the plant's defence system. As with all members of the onion family, garlic releases sulphurous compounds, predominantly allicin, when it is nibbled by an inquisitive animal, ensuring that only an initial munch is taken rather than a more comprehensive feasting. We take advantage of this release of allicin as the welcome taste and aroma we know as 'garlic' in our kitchens, but it is also responsible for many of the benefits that garlic is famous for – being antibacterial, blood-thinning, spirit-lifting, cholesterol-lowering, and detoxifying.

Legend has it that garlic also bestows upon those that eat it a lucky charm, protection and good fortune; it discourages the devil, and even returns lost souls. It's pretty good to cook with too.

Varieties

There are many reasons not to bother with growing your own garlic. It is easily sourced, cheap to buy and keeps well, but growing your own can give you access to more varieties, to fresh (or 'green') garlic, and you get the added bonus of its beneficial properties as a companion plant. 'Printanor' and 'Thermidrome' are good reliable varieties that should do as well as any in this country.

Although botanically closer to a leek than true garlic, 'Elephant' is definitely worth trying. Eaten green, it's a real treat, or you can roast it to bring out its full mild sweetness. It lives up to its name too, growing up to a hefty 10cm across.

A word of warning: don't bother trying to grow from cloves you've bought in the shops as most are grown in warm climes overseas and are prone to viruses that properly sourced garlic isn't.

How to grow

Garlic loves the sun and a free-draining patch, and it can be planted as a companion to ward off a range of nuisances, including carrot fly. You will buy either individual cloves or a whole head of garlic. If the latter, then separate the cloves, discarding the tiny ones at the centre. Plant them direct in October/November ideally, or in February/March, and they'll all be ready for harvesting in the summer. The

Garlic 'Printanor'

autumn-sown garlic, however, will be larger and slightly earlier to your kitchen than the ones sown later. Pop them in around 7cm deep (a little deeper for 'Elephant') with the flat base downwards, allowing around 15cm between them, with rows at least 20cm apart.

Garlic loves to flower, so if you are after a good-sized bulb, cut off the stem as it heads skywards in order to concentrate the plant's energies towards developing good bulbs.

How to harvest

Harvest time really depends on you. Pull the plants from June as green garlic for immediate use, or wait a while until any leaves yellow to investigate whether it's time to dig your garlic up. Once pulled, dry them in the sun for a day or two, then store indoors somewhere cool. Most varieties will last for around 4 months or so.

Problems and pests

As with other members of the onion family, rust (see p.98) can be a problem; crop rotation is your best prevention.

How to eat

Using garlic raw (crushed or chopped) makes the most of its beneficial qualities, as cooking diminishes them to a degree. Remember: the finer you chop, the stronger the flavour.

Roasted garlic is a delicious addition to many other dishes. Place a whole bulb in a small roasting tin, drizzle with olive oil and roast in the oven at 170°C/Gas Mark 3 for about 40 minutes. Squeeze out the soft, sweet pulp from the papery skins and stir into soups, dressings or sauces, or simply spread on toasted sourdough and top with soft cheese and roasted tomatoes.

Green garlic is altogether sweeter and gentler than its pungent relative, remaining in the background, yet enhancing its cooking pot companions to delicious effect. The late-spring/early-summer harvests – broad beans, lamb, artichokes, new potatoes and peas, in particular – take really well to green garlic. It's difficult to overuse, so don't be shy with it.

For more recipes, see pp.225, 227, 228, 229, 230, 234, 240, 242, 254, 257, 259.

Globe artichoke 'Romanesco'

Globe artichokes *Cynara scolymus*

PLANT GROUP	Perennials (see p.169)
START UNDER COVER	February–March
PLANT OUT	May–June
HARVEST	May–September

You'll end up with more on your plate after you've eaten a globe artichoke than was there to start with. Somehow piles of green material appear seemingly endlessly from this tight spiky ball. This deconstruction is inspired by the search for every scrap of the delicate nutty flesh that hides at the base of each petal, and at the heart of the flower itself. And it's well worth the effort – this is gourmet food for the lazy gardener – sow artichokes once, and they'll keep on giving harvest after harvest.

Globe artichokes tick all the right boxes – they are low maintenance, reliable croppers, easy to start off, have unbelievable flavour, and they are expensive in the shops. *And* this Mediterranean perennial is a looker. It can grow over 2 metres tall, bringing some wonderful structure to the plot, and throwing out delicious buds. If left to flower, these attract a whole range of beneficial insects, particularly bees, into the garden. The globe artichoke even makes a wonderful cut flower.

Varieties

Don't bother with the new varieties, which are geared very much towards commercial production. In my experience, they don't have the flavour of the older established varieties. 'Gros de Laon' and the purply 'Violetta di Chioggia' are a brilliant combination, or try 'Romanesco'. If you live in the North, then you may appreciate the extra hardiness of the 'Green Globe' variety.

How to grow

Sow under cover in Jiffy 7s (see p.197) or in modules in early spring – germination is usually quick. Pot on seedlings as soon as they are large enough to handle. Plant them out a pace or so apart in a sunny, well-drained spot in May or thereabouts.

During the first year, don't be tempted to let your taste buds get the better of you. Let the plant establish, and cut off any buds as soon as you see them. This will concentrate the plant's energies on developing its root system.

As for maintenance, it really couldn't be simpler. Add compost in winter as a mulch that will work its way into the ground and enrich the soil for the spring. And although some gardeners cut back the old stems to ground level in autumn, frankly I've never bothered. The plants will tire after 4 or 5 years, so you'll need new ones to take their place. Small plants, known as offsets, form at the base of the plant.

Select ones that are at least 30cm tall, with a couple of shoots and reasonable roots, and carefully detach them. Some people prefer to pot these offsets on for a year before planting out, but to my mind, that's an unnecessary step. I plant mine straight out, chop the leaves down by about half and water them well. I find they soon establish, ready to crop the year after.

How to harvest
The yield can be variable, but if you bank on getting eight or so globes from each plant every July–August you shouldn't be disappointed. Mediterranean they may be, but you can get a very long season if you're lucky. We've even picked them on Christmas Day, and some favour these winter treats. During the colder months the artichokes may be darker than usual or 'winter-kissed' – blistered white by the frost – but they should still be delicious and tender if they are green on the inside of the petals. Dodge any that are mouldy, drying out or wilting.

Problems and pests
None.

How to eat
Artichokes, if you're new to them, look as though they could do some damage in the wrong hands, and it's certainly not obvious how one cooks and eats them, so here's a crash course: firstly boil the globes whole until tender, which can take anything from 15–45 minutes depending on their size. To test, pull a leaf away from the base of the stem – it should come away easily. Once that's done, it's time to choose how you want to eat them.

The classic way to serve artichokes is whole, just boiled as they are, ready for guests to tear off the petals, dip in vinaigrette or melted, salted butter and strip the succulent flesh off from the base of each petal with their teeth.

Alternatively, once cooked you can strip all the petals off and chop out the hairy choke (the immature flower) to get to the fleshy heart that lies underneath. This succulent prized part is delicious with any number of dressings, or it can be preserved in oil, but my favourite way to eat it is made into houmous (see p.229) and served on crostini.

Catch artichokes young and small and try them raw, dipping each tender petal into your favourite dressing, without the fiddle of cooking or dealing with the choke. You can even braise these small artichokes to eat whole.

For more recipes, see pp.242, 244, 250.

Herbs

PLANT GROUP   Others (see p.169)

Herbs deserve a River Cottage Handbook of their own, so rather than attempt to be exhaustive I'm focusing on a few favourites. These are the herbs, well known and less so, that do their main job better than all the others, adding value to good produce, turning healthy harvests into great meals. Many also work well as companion plants (see p.212) and/or bring beneficial insects to your veg patch. Do try to grow at least a few, as you really can't afford to do without them – either out in the garden or in your kitchen.

There is much variety when it comes to spacing and timing of sowing. Check the seed packet and catalogue and follow the advice.

Herbs fall into two groups: the annuals, generally leafy, that you sow, grow and use within a year; and the perennials, generally woody, that will keep on giving over a longer period. I tend to grow the annual herbs scattered around the veg plot (although many gardeners prefer a dedicated bed for them). You can keep tender annuals going for at least some of the winter by bringing them indoors if they're in pots. I use the low-growing perennial herbs oregano and thyme to edge paths. A combination of cold and damp will kill off many herbs, so avoid such locations.

Perennials

Most of the woodier perennial herbs are from southern Europe, so give them what they're used to – sunny, drier, sheltered sites in well-drained soil. Add sand, grit and/or organic matter if your soil isn't up to scratch, but don't be tempted to compensate for the poor soil with feeds for the perennial herbs – they like it tough, and they'll only produce lush and more weakly flavoured growth. Perennials like to be divided in early spring. Prune them in March and don't be afraid to be fairly brutal, they'll bounce back with healthy new growth.

Bay *Laurus nobilis* An essential in any stock, stew or soup, bay brings a wonderfully aromatic edge that's surprisingly good in rice pudding too. Although expensive to buy as plants, it's the best way to start. You'll be repaid by endless leaves and the plant itself gets hardier as it ages, growing ever more vigorously to tree size if allowed. Any fish, whether baked, grilled, fried or barbecued, will benefit from a few leaves.

Chives *Allium schoenoprasum* These grow easily from seed, or you can divide existing plants. The best leaves come from young plants, so give yourself fresh plants at least every other year. Chives are an exception to most perennial herbs, favouring a good, rich, moist soil. They also do really well in pots and are fine grown indoors

Bay

Chives in flower

Moroccan mint

Oregano

for winter use. Their long thin leaves add a mild oniony bite to salads, fish dishes and soups, but do try the flowers as they're also delicious in salads. After flowering, cut chives back hard and you may well get a decent second flush of growth. Garlic chives, tasting as you'd imagine, are a variation well worth trying too.

Lemon verbena *Aloysia triphylla* The truly mouthwatering, cleansing smell of lemon that comes off these leaves is magnified by steeping them in boiled water. Lemon verbena can be a touch sensitive to the cold, so mulch around the roots with straw or similar, and to protect them through the winter – the plant will regrow when things warm up again. Water regularly and prune back hard in preparation for winter. The plant also does very well grown in pots. Fresh lemon verbena leaves are incredible; if dried, the leaves last and last. Use them to make a lovely refreshing tea, as the base for lemonade, and scattered over fruit salads.

Lovage *Levisticum officinale* A lesser-known and much-underrated herb, tasting a little like celery, lovage is an excellent addition to vegetable stock and many other recipes. It grows well from root propagation and seed, as long as you keep it moist and give it some room to grow. If you're growing it in a pot, make sure it's a good-sized one. Try it (sparingly at first) as a partner to peas, lettuce or potatoes in soup. For an amazing sauce that goes with just about any meat but is particularly special with pork: melt 2 tbsp butter in a pan, add 12 finely chopped lovage leaves, and cook for 3–4 minutes – don't worry if they turn dark green. Add a good splash of white wine and let it all simmer for a minute or two. Stir in 1 tsp wholegrain mustard and season well.

Mint *Menthe* sp. Another essential for your patch, although keep it in pots or otherwise restricted as it's very invasive. Try growing a few varieties as they all have their strengths – Moroccan makes the finest tea, peppermint's a great all-rounder, and spearmint is slightly milder than the rest. Mint favours a moist soil and does best in sun, but it will do okay in shade too.

Oregano *Origanum vulgare* An absolute must in a Bolognese sauce and many Mediterranean dishes. You can grow either tender or hardy varieties. Both are delicious, but the tender ones are usually fuller flavoured, while the hardy ones live longer. As with thyme, oregano is no problem to grow and look after, bringing bees and butterflies on to your patch. Give them a sunny site.

Rosemary *Rosmarinus officinalis* Rosemary is slow-growing, so it's understandably tempting to buy in plants to enable you to begin harvesting immediately. These can be expensive, however, so it may be a good idea to sow at least some of the plants you'll want. Once established, you'll get year-round aromatic leaves to go with your lamb, pasta sauces, roasted root veg, and anything else that will take this robust herb. Rosemary grows perfectly happily in a pot, so even if your space is limited, do try to grow at least one plant. As well as the flavoursome spiky leaves, the strikingly beautiful blue flowers bring the bees to your garden.

Sage *Salvia officinalis* Sage grows well from seed or from cuttings, lasting perhaps 5 years (though less in pots) before you need to replace them. Prune them back hard in spring to promote good strong growth, and don't be tempted to feed or water this sun lover. Little trouble to grow, you should get an all-year harvest to go perfectly with your pork, or to make tea that apparently refreshes the memory.

Tarragon *Artemisia dracunculus* A classic aniseedy herb, not to my mind at its best straight up, but wonderful in combination with receptive partners – classically with chicken, mayonnaise and fish. Grow sweet, punchy French tarragon, rather than the more bitter, tougher Russian variety. Divide or sow new plants every 3 years, and don't attempt tarragon in pots – it hates them.

This herb is worth growing if only to make your own tarragon vinegar: wash and chop 6 good handfuls of tarragon leaves and throw them into a large bowl. Pour in 1 litre white wine vinegar and decant into a large sterilised jar. Leave the jar on a sunny windowsill for a month or so, shaking it occasionally. Then pour the vinegar through muslin and decant into sterilised bottles or jars. Add a small fresh sprig of tarragon to each and seal.

Thyme *Thymus* sp. An aromatic low-growing herb that couldn't be easier to grow. There are endless varieties to try, but start with common thyme (*T. vulgaris*). It germinates and develops well from seed, and doesn't need watering other than during a drought. Plants will eventually tire though, and should be replaced every 5 years or so. Thyme doesn't really like growing indoors, so if you want some to hand, try a pot on an outside window ledge or by the back door. Beyond the beautiful aromatic flavour it lends to many dishes, thyme has another advantage: bees love the flowers and will pollinate lots of other plants for you while they're about.

Annuals

The annuals tend to prefer things more moist, the soil richer, a little shade, and with plenty of room to develop and to ensure air circulation. Generally they grow easily from seed, and as a result are inexpensive. If you prepare a good bed, adding organic matter, you'll get them off to a good start and have every chance of unchecked progress. Quick growth is what you are after for succulent leaves, so unless otherwise suggested for your variety, don't let them dry out, and give them the odd comfrey feed (see p.215) to top up nutrients if you're growing them in containers. Unlike most perennial herbs, the majority of annuals deteriorate rapidly after picking, so pick them as you need them, and if there's any wait at all, pop their stems in a jar of water.

Basil *Ocimum basilicum* You'll find numerous varieties of this aromatic classic, but start with 'Sweet Genovese' as your main crop around which to experiment. Basil is the smell of summer to many, making an excellent companion for tomatoes in the kitchen and in the garden. Sow seed thinly from spring, planting out after frosts if you've started them in modules, and ensure you don't let your basil dry out. In your veg patch basil can be a little hit and miss, even in the summer, but it's easy to grow under cover, doing well in pots. If you want to extend your harvest, cut back your plants before flowering to encourage fresh growth. Pesto (see p.258) is the obvious avenue for any surplus, although you can freeze leaves whole in oil – in ice cube trays – to pull the scent of summer into the autumn and winter.

Chervil *Anthriscus cerefolium* If you're new to chervil, its taste is something like parsley with a slight hint of aniseed. As you can imagine, that makes it excellent in salads, with fish and in many sauces. Happiest in shade, doing well in pots, chervil should not be allowed to dry out. Sow direct from early spring until autumn and you should get a harvest in most months.

Coriander *Coriandrum sativum* With its amazing leaves, followed later by wonderful seeds, coriander will give you two essential harvests. Sow seeds in April and May, give them a rich soil and water them only in a drought. The leaves add a pungent freshness to salads, salsas, curries and other dishes, while the seeds lend a light aromatic spiciness to meat and fish dishes, as well as a punchy spike to bread.

Dill *Anethum graveolens* A delicious, though much underused herb, dill is essential for gravadlax, and outstanding with poached fish, cucumber, gherkins and potatoes. Sow direct or in pots in spring, don't water unless there's a really dry patch, and don't cut it back as it sulks. Dill is one of those herbs that the more you eat it, the more you want to eat it, so pinch the odd bit as you're walking around your veg patch and you'll find you come up with endless possibilities for it. It's fantastic in dressings and sauces for most seafood, chicken and cool crunchy lettuces.

Parsley *Petroselinum crispum* You can choose between curly and flat-leaved parsley; the latter has slightly more flavour. Although usually treated as an annual, parsley will often survive all year round, though I've found to get the best leaves you should replace the plants after 6 or 7 months. Sow direct, only just covering the seeds with soil, and keep them from drying out. And sow a lot... you'll use it.

Jerusalem artichokes

Helianthus tuberosus

PLANT GROUP	Perennials (see p.169)
SOW DIRECT	January–March
HARVEST	October–March

Some plants should be in every veg patch and this is one. Where else would you get a beautiful late-summer cut flower, a seasonal windbreak, kilos of compostable material, and – as if that wasn't enough – a delicious, yet underrated food year after year? And all for doing little other than planting them once.

Contrarily, they are neither artichoke nor from Jerusalem, but a sunflower originally named girasole after the Italian for sunflower. Girasole gradually morphed into Jerusalem, but their apparent similarity in taste to the globe artichoke that spawned the rest of their name is one that passes me by. To my palate, this veg has a wonderfully savoury flavour that shouts out its origins in the earth.

With a leafy, flowering stem that can reach 3 metres, Jerusalem artichokes are a tasty root, high in potassium, iron, fibre and endless other vitamins and minerals, so why are they comparatively uncommon? Perhaps it is their reputation for digestive disturbance. In *Gerard's Herbal* of 1621, John Goodyer observed that they 'cause a filthy loathsome stinking wind within the body, thereby causing the belly to be pained and tormented, and are a meat more fit for swine than men'. An exaggeration perhaps, but there's no denying their gas-giving qualities do affect some. Fortunately the more frequently eaten, the more effectively the body deals with the starch. That's not only cause for celebration among sufferers (and their companions), but also an invitation to eat more of this unappreciated vegetable.

Varieties

There are a few varieties about but 'Fuseau' is the one to go for. Less knobbly than most others and therefore less grief in preparing, it has an outstanding flavour.

How to grow

In early spring, plant the tubers direct, 15cm down and 60cm apart, in a permanent bed, or plant them as a windbreak... and wait. By mid-summer they'll throw up stems, slowly forming sunflower-like heads that burst open towards the end of September. Let the frosts hit them to kill off the flowers that you haven't cut for decorating the house and (as with parsnips) the chill will improve the flavour of the tubers. You may have heard of the potential for Jerusalem artichokes to become invasive. As with raspberries, the notion of a self-expanding harvest sounds like a bonus to me, but if you prefer things neat and tidy, beware of their lateral creep.

How to harvest
The artichokes will be ready to harvest from October through to May, depending on when you sow. They store unreliably, so dig them when you're about to use them, leaving a few tubers for next year's growth. In practice it's pretty hard not to leave some behind. Each of your planted tubers should return around 2kg of delicious artichokes for eating.

Problems and pests
None.

How to eat
Smooth-skinned tubers, such as 'Fuseau', can be simply washed thoroughly before use, whereas knobblier varieties are best par-boiled, refreshed with cold water and rubbed to remove their skins. They make an amazing soup (see p.227), the perfect vegetable crisps, and take to the roasting tin especially well. Yet my favourite way to eat them is finely sliced, softened in a pan with butter, then blitzed with cream and stirred at the last minute into risotto. For more recipes, see pp.238, 253.

Jerusalem artichokes 'Fuseau'

Kale *Brassica oleracea* var. *acephala*

PLANT GROUP	Brassicas (see p.159)
START UNDER COVER	March–August
PLANT OUT	April–September
HARVEST	June–February

It would be hard to find a lower-maintenance, yet more highly nutritious and flavourful leaf that offers such variety. From the robust, dark 'Cavalo Nero' to the more delicate 'Red Russian', picked for baby salad, you're spoilt for choice. If you're pushed for space and have to prioritise, make sure kale makes the cut.

Varieties
'Cavalo Nero', 'Red Russian', 'Redbor' (F1), and 'Walking Stick' kale are all worth growing. They're very different in appearance and taste, yet equally delicious.

How to grow
Sow in March for summer picking, or as late as August for autumn and winter harvesting. Start them off under cover in Jiffy 7s (see p.197) or modules if you're after full-sized plants, or sow in guttering if you want cut-and-come-again leaves. Plant out as little as 10cm apart for the latter, to around 50cm for plants to reach full size. They are slowish to mature, long at their peak and keep producing if you pick leaves, so two or three sowings over the year should give you constant kale.

How to harvest
Expect to harvest kale leaves 3–4 months after sowing. If it's variety you're after, adopt a cut-and-come-again approach. 'Red Russian' is perfect for planting closely and picking the leaves when only a few centimetres long – toss raw into salads.

Problems and pests
Cabbage white butterflies can be a pain in spring and summer. I find companion planting (see p.212) and picking off the caterpillars prevents any real harm, but you could try 'Pentland Brig' and 'Redbor' as these seem less attractive to them.

How to eat
Use kale in any recipes that are suited to cabbage or Brussels sprouts. For a great pasta sauce: steam the leaves until tender; drain, chop finely and throw into a pan with some olive oil and garlic for a few minutes. Add a touch of cream – and chilli, herbs, capers, Parmesan etc, as you prefer. For more recipes, see pp.223, 242, 255.

Kale 'Pentland Brig'

Leeks 'Hannibal'

Leeks *Allium ampeloprasum* var. *porrum*

PLANT GROUP	Onions (see p.164)
START UNDER COVER	February–April
PLANT OUT	June–July
HARVEST	September–May (earlier for baby leeks)

Grow leeks once and you'll become attached very quickly. They are delicious, versatile veg that make the plot look special even through the cold months when the frosts are around. There's something about that almost algal green-blue that just suits the cold.

With a good selection of early and late varieties, you can harvest from September through winter and into early spring, adding to your arsenal of 'hungry gap' fillers. You can even add a month or two on at the early part of your harvest by growing some of your leek seedlings just a little longer instead of transplanting them. Pick these when they are just the size of spring onions for a late-summer treat.

Do leave a few plants to flower through late spring and into the summer. Extraordinarily beautiful, they add the third dimension to the plot, keeping a satisfying connection with what has been, and providing you with all the seed you need for the coming year.

Varieties
'Monstruoso de Carentan' (early), 'D'Hiver de Saint-Victor' (late), 'Saint Victor' (late) and 'Musselburgh' (late) are delicious, reliable yearly fixtures in my veg garden, and having tried 'Hannibal' as an early variety for the first time I've a feeling it will be making a return. 'King Richard', a very early variety, is particularly excellent for baby leeks.

How to grow
Start early- or late-harvesting leek varieties in guttering under cover in March–April, sowing 3cm apart. Plant out in June or July, in the roots/onions patch or to follow your early spuds if you have lifted them.

Planting out is quite a particular process: tease the leek, which should be 20cm or so tall, out of the guttering; trim its roots to 5cm; make a hole 15cm deep with a pencil and lower the leek gently into it. Keep the plants at a distance of around 15cm from their neighbours, in rows 30cm apart. Fill the holes with water, but don't infill with soil.

Baby leeks are well worth adding to your summer menu. Sow them thinly and successionally – a few weeks apart – in a bed with a very fine tilth. Thin the emerging seedlings, allowing 3cm between them. It is important to water baby leeks frequently.

If you are after a larger ratio of white to green, you can always earth your leeks up a little, or even set the seedlings into slightly deeper holes.

Problems and pests
Rust, evident as orange or brown blotches on the leaves, can affect your harvest but usually only decoratively. The odd seaweed or comfrey feed (see p.215) helps prevent it, but rotating your crops strictly (see p.172) is the main way of minimising any problem with rust. If you do have a more serious infection, dig up all affected plants and burn them.

How to harvest
Harvest leeks as you need them from September onwards, or in the case of baby leeks, when they are pencil-thick and look very much like spring onions.

If you're leaving some to flower (which you really must) you can always save the seed for the following harvest. Be aware that they won't replicate the original variety unless that is the only variety you are growing.

How to eat
Leeks lend a wonderful base flavour to any number of soups, most famously the classic vichyssoise (creamed leek and potato), which is traditionally served cold, but equally delicious hot. They are also excellent in stews, pies, pasta sauces, risottos and stir-fries.

Most recipes call mainly for the milder white part of the veg, but don't discard the green part. Instead use it to flavour stocks and marinades, or to add flavour to a roast chicken pop a piece of green leek into the cavity with a wedge of lemon and some parsley stalks.

Where a recipe calls for whole leeks, these can be a bit tricky to clean. The easiest way is to slit them along the length of the green part at intervals, then immerse in cold water to tease out the soil.

Try steaming small or medium leeks until just tender, then hit them with olive oil, a little lemon juice and some chopped parsley for a lovely side dish or light lunch. Baby leeks are even better friends with cream and sage. Steam or griddle them to bring a wonderfully intense leekiness into your summer. For more recipes, see pp.227, 228, 248.

Lettuces *Lactuca sativa*

PLANT GROUP	Salad leaves (see p.166)
START UNDER COVER	January–September
PLANT OUT	April–October
SOW DIRECT	March–September
HARVEST	All year

Generally high-yielding and easy to grow, lettuces offer a fantastic variety of colour, texture and taste. They also reward a little careful investigation. Most of us think of lettuces as either tight cones (hearting lettuce) or slack-headed roses (loose-leaf lettuce), which of course they can be, but there is another way of getting the most from them. As well as letting some lettuces develop fully, we can also tuck in a little earlier by treating the lettuce bed as a salad orchard. Pluck a few young leaves here and there and in a few short weeks they'll regrow for another harvest – a cycle of cut-and-come-again cropping that can last for months.

By nipping off a few leaves from different varieties of lettuce you'll also be opening up all sorts of mixed salad possibilities for the table. Add in edible flowers (see p.72), oriental leaves (see p.105), herbs (see p.87) and other leaves such as rocket, and this really is one area of your harvest where you can let your imagination run riot.

Varieties

Lettuces love the sun but they like it cool too, so if you're happy to put in a little effort, and you go for the right varieties, you can grow lettuce all year round, enjoying a different leafy salad every day of the year.

For summer and autumn harvesting: 'Little Gem' is a classic. This fast-growing cos lettuce is a must for every patch and perfect for container growing, followed closely by 'Pinokkio', which makes an excellent (some say superior) alternative.

For winter and spring harvesting: 'Marvel of Four Seasons' lives up to its name deliciously, while 'Winter Density', 'Rouge d'Hiver' and the soft-headed 'Valdor' are all good varieties. And from 'Green Oak Leaf', you can pluck perfect cut-and-come-again leaves right through winter.

How to grow

Getting a steady harvest rather than a glut is the key with lettuces and there are some simple ways of ensuring a good succession: sow every few weeks; every time you sow, start some off direct and others under cover in modules as they'll mature at different times; and if you grow some for leaf supply and let others develop hearts from the same sowing you'll have an automatic successional harvest. Plant out

Lettuce Winter Density

Planting Date

Lettuce 'Winter Density'

those sown in modules when 5–10 cm tall. Spacing is very flexible. Sow close for cut-and-come-again leaves (maximising your yield per area and minimising bare soil) or further apart (check the packet) if you're growing them to full maturity.

For spring and summer lettuces, sow under cover from New Year and outside in your patch from March. Lettuces like sunny yet cooler conditions for germination, so beware the hottest weeks (mid-June to mid-August) as they'll tend to bolt. Sow in the evening and water the ground first at this time of year. Give summer lettuces a shady spot, don't let them dry out, and treat them as cut-and-come-agains – to avoid them going to seed in the heat.

For leaves through winter into spring, sow in late summer and autumn (check the catalogue or seed packet for times). They'll do better under cover but with luck you may be successful outside, especially if you give them a little fleece protection.

Keep an eye on your lettuces as they start to heart – usually around 3 months after sowing. Given half a chance, too much sun and/or too little water they'll happily bolt, which makes most varieties taste bitter. Water regularly during this delicate time. But don't overwater winter lettuces – indeed, you may not need to water them at all.

Keep plants well weeded – lettuces hate competition.

How to harvest
One of those essential foods that you can harvest every day. Taking a cut-and-come-again approach to at least some of your lettuces will enable you to get the most from your plot. Either pick up to half of the young leaves, or cut them all 3 cm or so above ground, and in a few short weeks they'll grow back.

Problems and pests
You'll not be the only one after these succulent, tender leaves – slugs and snails will need to be deterred (see p.216). Bolting in the summer months is also a risk, lessened by taking a cut-and-come-again approach and watering well in dry periods.

How to eat
For the most part, lettuce isn't a flavourfest. Most varieties are neutral, but that's not to say they are flavourless. The differences are often subtle but they are present, awaiting a simple dressing of good oil and salt, or (for a crispy cos) griddling. Good on their own, they also make the perfect mixed salad base, a platform on which smaller amounts of the more exhibitionist leaves can play.

And if the idea of salad in December doesn't appeal, firstly give it a whirl – you may be surprised; and secondly try lettuce cooked. It makes a marvellous risotto (chopped and wilted into the rice for the last few minutes of cooking) and a clean, refreshing soup (see p.226). For more recipes, see pp.238, 248, 250.

Onions *Allium cepa*

PLANT GROUP	Onions (see p.164)
SOW DIRECT	Seed or sets March–April, or September–October for sets of overwintering varieties
HARVEST	May–October

Most of us use onions every day so they are a prime candidate for inclusion in your veg patch, but don't sacrifice your valuable space without some judicious selection. I grow only a few white maincrop onions in the summer, because they are cheap to buy, locally available, store for a long period and take up a fair amount of the veg patch at the busiest time of the growing year.

Instead I give priority to the sweetness of shallots and red onions, and the punch of spring onions (see p.135). Red varieties and shallots are no more trouble to grow than their white cousins, and are inexplicably expensive to buy. So if you're in any way short of space, knock a hole in your food budget by growing these onions and shop for the white ones. You also have the option of growing your white varieties over winter, taking up room when there's likely to be less in your veg patch and giving you a springtime harvest.

Varieties

Delicious and reliable, 'Red Baron' is the outstanding red onion. 'Stoccarde' is a tasty, reliable white main cropper, and 'Radar' is worth a go if you're after a reliable overwintering white onion.

How to grow

Most onions can be grown from either seed or mini-onions known as sets. Sets are easier to deal with, but seed is considerably cheaper if you're going for a big harvest.

Plant maincrop sets during the first half of spring, and overwintering varieties in September or October. For both, the tips should be just slightly below the level of the soil. The rule of closeness and harvest size applies: plant 4–10cm apart for small onions; or 15–25cm apart for larger ones.

With seed, sow direct in early spring – thinly in lines, 1cm deep and 15cm apart. You are likely to have to thin the seedlings, spacing them according to the size of onion you are after.

Although reasonably low maintenance, onions do like a sunny, well-drained spot... they'll happily run to seed if they get the opposite. Also, make sure your onions are clear of weeds. This enables your crop to get the nutrients it needs, and ensures good airflow around the bulbs, minimising the risk of disease.

Onions drying before storing
'Red Baron' and 'Sturon Globe'

How to harvest

As onions mature, the leaves will start to yellow and at this stage you can bend the tops over to aid ripening. Lift your onions when you like the size they are. You should be pulling larger maincrop onions from mid-summer. Leave them to dry for a day or two in the sun, then store them somewhere light for up to around 6 months. An ideal airy way to store them until you're ready to use them is in pairs of tights, knotted between the bulbs. Start using them from the toe end, snipping below each knot as you go. Overwintering onions don't store for long so pull them as needed, don't bother with drying, and use them immediately.

Problems and pests

Onion downy mildew and white rot are possible problems, though not overly common. You can't do much about it if you encounter either of these, but rotating your crops (see p.172) is vital to minimising the likelihood.

Neck rot, should it occur, is more likely to be visible in stored onions. Sort through your harvest well before storing, discarding any that are soft, and use any that seem borderline straight away.

How to eat

Preparing onions may not be the most popular kitchen task, but the chemical that causes eye-stinging is released (mainly from the leafier end) to protect the plant from being munched by pests as it grows. If you hold the leafier end, chop off the bottom of your onion and slice from that end, you'll reduce those tears.

As well as all the everyday uses, onions are really worthy of a starring role. French onion soup and onion tart are deserving classics, but if you've a glut – of red onions especially – try making them into a tasty preserve.

Red onion marmalade is my favourite companion to sausages, goes brilliantly with cheese, and couldn't be easier to make: peel and slice 1kg red onions and slowly fry them in a little sunflower oil, stirring once in a while, until they are quite soft. Turn the heat up to quickly drive off any moisture and pour in 80ml red wine vinegar and 100g soft brown sugar. Continue to cook, stirring more frequently, until the mixture thickens and becomes a touch sticky. For extra bite, stir through 1–2 tsp wholegrain mustard, if you like. Spoon into sterilised, airtight jars, refrigerate and use within a month or two.

For more recipes, see pp.223, 225, 227, 228, 247, 248, 256, 259.

Oriental leaves

PLANT GROUP	Others (see p.169)

There are so many outstanding oriental leaves, and so much flexibility about when to grow and harvest, and how to use them, that the best I can offer is an introduction to the indispensable favourites – the rest is up to your sense of inquisitiveness. They can do much to liven up your kitchen, particularly during the leaner weeks.

How to grow

Many oriental leaves are happily sown and grown in full sun. Follow your catalogue/ seed packet advice, as even varieties of the same plant can be grown differently. These leaves will give you tasty harvests from the end of summer through to early December outside, and right through winter if grown under cover. Most develop quickly, giving you a fast return, but they will ask for water to maintain unchecked growth. Pests love them too, so try growing most of your oriental leaves later in the year – to follow on from peas, beans and lettuce. Through the winter you may not get excessive growth but you can still pinch off a small harvest, and as soon as there's a hint of warmth you'll find new leaves to perk up the lean weeks.

I tend to start some off under cover in modules, and sow some direct under cover and outside. This provides a succession in harvest and some insurance should pests make hay in the outdoor leaves or if some run to seed. Spacings vary considerably, so follow what it says on the packet. Nearly all the oriental leaves do well from a cut-and-come-again approach – it ensures you get a harvest early and tender, and stimulates more growth. When harvesting, pick the leaves when you want to eat them, as many deteriorate rapidly once picked, and it's usually better to cut with small, sharp scissors as many are shallow-rooting and are easily dislodged. All of this wonderful group will do well in containers or on your windowsill.

Varieties

Confusingly, lots of oriental leaves are sold under more than one name, and/or have different spellings. Also, many are sold as generic rather than named varieties, so be guided by catalogue/packet descriptions, and source seed from a good supplier.

Amaranth This nutritious leaf is used all over the world; it is particularly popular eaten as calaloo in the Caribbean and horta in Greece. Also known as Chinese spinach, the taste is somewhere between spinach and artichoke and you can use it in the same ways as spinach – particularly when small and young for salads, or wilted with lemon juice and olive oil. It has the advantage of being slow to bolt, even when grown in the hottest months when many others want to run to seed.

Chop suey greens Often sold under this generic name, but also as the superior 'Shungiku' variety, these are very easy to grow. When the plant reaches 15cm or so, only 6 or 7 weeks after sowing, you get beautiful aromatic leaves to add variety and punch to salads, or to sauté with bacon and serve as a side veg through all but the coldest months. And you can leave some to grow on as a bee-friendly flower, cutting some for the house.

Giant red mustard These vibrant crimson and green leaves make a stunning addition to your patch and your kitchen, providing a harvest into and right through the colder months. The larger you let the leaves grow, the hotter they get, adding a horseradishy hit to a beef sandwich in February. One of my favourite winter leaves.

Kai lan This is the first year I've grown this oriental leaf and I've found something special. It looks very much like a slightly less rufty-tufty sprouting broccoli, throwing up sweet succulent shoots through the warmer months. It needs next-to-no steaming, loves all the sauces and dressings you'd hope it would, and no matter how much you eat you never get tired of it. I'm genuinely wondering if this hasn't the potential to be the veg that makes up the fourth leg of the culinary relay, that starts with sprouting broccoli, asparagus and peas. It's that good.

Mibuna Untidy and with slightly rounder leaves and a milder flavour than mizuna (see below), mibuna will offer itself for salads, wilting and stir-fries all year. To get it at its best, avoid sowing this one in the hottest months as it may well bolt.

Mizuna Looking a little like wild rocket that's filled out, mizuna's delightfully scruffy leaves give you a not-too-intense mustardy addition, either raw in salads or cooked in any number of ways. Apart from the flavour, the best thing about mizuna is its year-round harvesting time.

Pak choi Mild, juicy and crisp, yet succulent when small, pak choi is a real must. It will also give you a quick return – mid-summer leaves within a month of planting. Add to mixed salads, eat raw on its own, toss into stir-fries or have as an alternative side veg to any leafy brassica. It is often sold as a generic variety, but 'Green Revolution' (F1) and 'China Choi' are particularly tasty, and reliably fast-growing.

Wong bok This is one of those Chinese cabbages that looks like a 'Little Gem' lettuce that's been to the gym. Maybe I'm just lazy, but there's something very appealing about a vegetable that keeps its prize tucked away from mud and doesn't need washing or fiddling with. Peel off its gloriously sweet crisp leaves to use in salads, or slice thinly and stir-fry.

Giant red mustard

Pak choi

Mibuna

Amaranth (foreground)

Parsnips *Pastinaca sativa*

PLANT GROUP	Roots (see p.162)
SOW DIRECT	March–May
HARVEST	August–March

Easy to grow, the parsnip is a fine source of fibre and rich in vitamins and minerals. It also loves a frost, turning its stored starches into more sugars, just waiting to come out with a slow roasting in your kitchen. It's shape may lend itself to showmanship, but don't be tempted to try and impress with the size of your parsnips, as woody, bland tapering roots will be your reward. Buy a sports car instead, and keep your parsnips small.

Varieties

'Tender and True' has a fantastic flavour, getting to a decent size (about 7cm across the shoulders) before edging anywhere near fibrous territory. This year I also grew 'Gladiator' (F1) and they were outstanding, giving me a heavy, deliciously sweet crop of unwoody parsnips.

How to grow

Parsnips prefer a sandy, loamy, well-worked soil. These are not veg for the impatient: slow to germinate and slow to grow, they can be in the ground for 10 months. Sow them direct in early spring in rows 30cm apart, thinning to 15cm between plants.

Parsnip seed deteriorates rapidly, so buy fresh each year. And don't add organic matter to the ground before sowing parsnips as they will probably fork.

How to harvest

Traditionally you start to harvest after the first frost and continue through winter, but you can keep the spacing smaller and harvest delicious baby roots in summer.

Problems and pests

Parsnips are usually trouble-free, though wireworm can be a problem. Keep your plants well weeded and dig over an affected area (see p.219).

How to eat

Parsnip's sweet, aromatic flesh adds comfort to many dishes. Roasted with honey (see p.253) or flavoured with warm spices, such as cumin and coriander, they are a treat. Try alternating them with spuds in dauphinoise potatoes (see p.254), or use them to replace carrots in a cake (see p.260). For more recipes, see pp.223, 225.

Parsnip 'Halblange White'

Peas *Pisum sativum*

PLANT GROUP	Legumes (see p.157)
START UNDER COVER	February–May
PLANT OUT	May–June
SOW DIRECT	October–November for overwintering varieties, and/or March–June
HARVEST	May–October

When he'd done with being President of the USA, Thomas Jefferson went back to tending his patch, and with such vigour and success that to many his greater achievement lies in his gardens at Monticello. He trialled endless varieties of any veg he could lay his hands on, but he wasn't such an anorak that he didn't know how to welcome in a harvest. Every year he held a competition to find the grower of the first peas of the season. The winner then invited all contestants to supper with the peas taking centre stage. There's far too little of this seasonal celebration going on now, so we've decided to reinstate the tradition here at River Cottage and encourage you to do likewise. I'm expecting inventive methods, underhand dealings and outright cheating.

Peas will take up a little of your time. Most will need support while they grow, and if you have a family gathering, you'll certainly find podding is best done by a few people. But time spent on peas is rarely better spent. I guarantee one taste of your home-grown own and they'll become a permanent fixture on your plot. As with asparagus, the speed of the conversion of their sugars to starches means that minutes count. If you can't eat them straight away, then get them cold or frozen as this arrests the loss of sweetness.

Personally I don't think it's worth buying fresh peas. At best they'll have been picked several days before, and frozen peas taken straight from the field to the freezer within a few hours generally have a much better taste. However, to fully appreciate the taste of fresh peas at their absolute peak, there really is no other way than growing your own. Once you've tasted them, most of your peas won't even make it to the pan as they are among the finest grazing treats you can award yourself as you go about some task or other. Treat them as sweets.

And it's not only the peas that you're after from your plants. The side shoots and growth tips, known as pea tips (or 'green gold' to the Japanese) will add a succulent, sweet crunch to any salad; they are also delightful eaten just as they are. You will end up with fewer pods if you pick them, but if you have a lot of plants or you've had more successful germinations than expected, grow the reserves on just for

Peas 'Purple Podded Pea'

these tips. You can even get an indoor crop of tips all year round by sowing some in autumn – to bring a touch of springtime zing to the darkest months.

As well as the pea we all know and love, you may want to try growing mangetout peas, which are eaten whole, as their name suggests. Or sugar snaps, which are eaten in the same way and have a lovely crunchy texture and delectable sweetness.

Varieties

Pea seed is sometimes sold as either wrinkle-seeded or round-seeded varieties. Both are good for spring sowing, but round varieties can also be sown in October–November to give an early harvest in May.

There are many excellent varieties but I've found 'Alderman', 'Douce Provence' (my favourite round-seeded variety) and 'Hurst Green Shaft' to be especially tasty, reliable and heavy-cropping. 'Purple Podded Pea' makes a stunning addition to the veg patch and tastes as good as it looks. If you can't wait to sample your fresh peas, try 'Kelvedon Wonder' – not only delicious, but very quick to crop (about 75 days from a spring sowing). 'Markana' is a good dwarf variety choice if your patch is exposed or you have limited space; it grows to only around 75cm and is reasonably self-supporting. Expect most pea varieties to mature in around 100 days.

And don't overlook sugar snaps (usually sold as generic 'sugar snap' rather than as named varieties), or mangetout – 'Norli' and 'Weggisser' are particularly tasty varieties. Try half a row of each as a taster and you'll soon be sowing more.

How to grow

Peas will do okay on most soils, but if you're after a fantastic crop, incorporate plenty of organic matter and dig the bed well, but don't be tempted to add manure. If you do, you'll get plenty of encouraging growth but a disappointing crop of peas.

It's best to start peas off under cover in root trainers or toilet roll inners (see p.197) to help them develop a healthy root run that should get them off to a fine start when planted out. Sow too many, to ensure you'll have enough backups should the birds or slugs invade, using any spares for pea tips. Plant them out when they are around 10–15cm tall.

If you want to sow straight into your plot, avoid doing so in wet, cold conditions as the seeds are likely to rot. Spacing varies with variety (check the packet) but allow around 10cm between plants and keep rows around 75cm apart.

To give you a long, steady season and avoid a huge glut, sow them successionally a fortnight apart, and pick them regularly – to encourage more pods to form.

The taller pea varieties will need some support. Twiggy hazel prunings, thrust fat end into the soil, are traditional and work best. These hold the plants upright and offer something for the growing tendrils to latch on to. The dwarf varieties tend to provide each other with mutual support to a degree, but you may have to supply a helping stick or two if they need it. As with climbing beans, the taller peas can easily make 2 metres tall, so avoid exposed areas of your plot, and be aware of any shadowing likely to result. Radishes and salad leaves are a top choice to fill any affected area, as they'll enjoy the shade.

Do keep your plants from drying out. The occasional comfrey feed (see p.215) from flowering will boost pea production a little, but it's not essential.

How to harvest

Many varieties reach harvest within 2 months and should be picked at their peak.

Problems and pests

Mice and birds love the seed, so start most, if not all, of your peas off under cover. This also helps get them past their most vulnerable stage, when slugs and snails are particularly damaging.

You're quite likely to see small stamp-edge notches appearing on the young spring leaves, caused by pea and bean weevils. This is rarely a problem as the damage is usually insignificant and your harvest will be unaffected. More frustratingly, the caterpillar of the pea moth goes about its business unseen, burrowing into the pod and your precious peas, yet visible only when you pop the pod to taste them. The best way to deal with this nuisance is to avoid it. The caterpillar hatches to enjoy its main feeding in July and early August, so time your sowings to mature before and after this period. Mangetout are unaffected as they are picked before the peas develop – use them as a mid-summer harvest between your early and late peas.

How to eat

Cook peas briefly (if at all) to enjoy them at their best, and do try Jane Grigson's suggestion for young and tender peas: boil them in their pods so the peas steam, plunge briefly in cold water and pick them up by the stalk, dip in butter (or any sauce you fancy), and suck out the peas, crunching the pods at the end.

If you miss peas when they are small and sweet, don't discard them. Pick the larger pods to encourage more to form and use their peas for purées, fritters, burgers and minty mushy peas.

Once you've shelled your peas, don't throw the pods away. Make 'compost soup': wash the pods, add them to a pan of boiling stock or water and simmer for 6–7 minutes, then throw in 8–12 washed outer lettuce leaves and continue to cook until the pods are soft. Purée in a blender or using a hand-held stick blender until smooth. Season with a pinch of sugar, salt and freshly ground black pepper. Serve with a spoon of yoghurt half stirred in. Apart from being delicious, there's the added satisfaction that much of it was otherwise destined for the compost heap.

For more recipes, see pp.223, 226, 229, 233, 237, 239, 244, 248, 258.

Peppers *Capsicum annuum*

PLANT GROUP	Solanaceae (see p.168)
START UNDER COVER	February–March
PLANT OUT	May–June
HARVEST	August–November

Last year I harvested two peppers, hardly enough to keep body and soul nourished, but they were spot on – sweet, edgy and bright. It was just enough of a carrot to get me trying once more. I've rarely had the success with sweet peppers that I have with their fiery cousins... perhaps I'm sending out signals that I prefer to eat chillies. But I do quite like peppers, enough to grow them for sure, not least because they have plenty of uses in the kitchen.

Even growing peppers in the Southwest, I have found them to be just short of the heat and light they crave to crop and ripen reliably to their peak. They are worth a try though, as they're wildly different from those you buy in supermarkets. And they are undoubtedly more successful grown in a greenhouse or polytunnel (or even on a windowsill) than out in the veg patch.

Varieties

I may have had limited success over the years, but I can tell you there's a world of difference between the best varieties and the rest. 'Californian Wonder', 'Marconi Rossa' and 'Sweet Nardello' are so good that even a miserable harvest will get you growing them in hope next year.

How to grow

Sow pepper seeds under cover in early March in Jiffy 7s (see p.197) or small pots. Keep them either on a bench or on a windowsill in the house as they'll love the extra warmth. Peppers need a long sunny season to mature, so don't start them off after April, otherwise they won't have time to get there.

Peppers can take a month to germinate. You can pop them in the airing cupboard to speed it up, but do get them out as soon as they start to emerge. Pot them into 9cm pots and on to larger ones when the roots start to poke out. Get them into the ground or into their final pot in June – and if you are after optimum results, grow them under cover.

As with chillies, peppers are less trouble to the grower than tomatoes, but less reliable in coming to full ripeness. Comfrey waterings (see p.215) or sprays given from flowering onwards are invaluable, but don't overwater them. Also, do tie the plants to a stake for support. It's also a good idea to limit the height (essential if

Pepper 'Marconi Rossa' early ripening

you're growing them in pots), so pinch out the growing tips to encourage them to bush out. Hand-pollinating the first flowers with a soft paint brush seems to improve the chances of getting more fruit.

How to harvest
Peppers vary in colour but many move through the classic green to red ripening process. You can pick them at any point along this timeline, even when small and green. Try one at each stage (snipping them off the brittle plant) and see how you prefer them. There is the added advantage that picking a few early in mid-summer will stimulate others to follow, ready through to early autumn.

Problems and pests
Pepper plants are rarely subject to any problems. If they are troubled by anything, it will most probably be aphids (see pp.217–18 for remedies).

How to eat
If you've had a half-decent pepper harvest, you deserve to celebrate it. Now you've grown them, you can see for yourself just what a revelation of sweet tender heaven they can be.

Roasting peppers is the best way to go with them: place in a roasting tin, drizzle with a little olive oil and roast in the oven at 190°C/Gas Mark 5 for half an hour or so until softened and a little charred. When they're ready, pop them hot into a polythene bag or seal them in a plastic container (anything that is airtight), for 5 minutes or so. This steams them slightly and makes it easy to slip the skins off. Once skinned, slit open the peppers and remove the core and seeds. Now they're ready to transform into rich, sweet soup – with the same weight of roasted tomatoes, good veg stock and a little chilli for punch. Alternatively, cut into strips and scatter over pizzas (see p.242) or into salads to add sweetness and colour.

Fortunately peppers are robust enough to keep their shape and substance when roasted crammed full of all manner of stuffings: capers, olives, anchovies, garlic, aubergines, tomatoes – really anything with a Mediterranean touch works well.

For more recipes, see pp.230, 233, 244, 256.

Potatoes *Solanum tuberosum*

PLANT GROUP	Solanaceae (see p.168)
SOW DIRECT	February–April
HARVEST	May–October

Dedicate your space to the truly delicious, less common potato varieties and you'll find them one of the crops that really passes the home-grown taste test. Most of the varieties named below are waxy, flavoursome and less widely available in the shops, and I'd urge you to concentrate on growing these.

Unless you do not have a local supplier you can buy from, or you have more space than you need, or you are aiming for self-sufficiency – and you can live with the frequent disappointment of blight – then I'd urge you not to bother with many (if any) maincrop bakers or mashers. New potatoes and some late-season waxy varieties are not only amazing to eat, they're expensive to buy in the shops. Prioritise these and your pocket will notice the difference, as well as your taste buds.

The exception to the maincrop rule is the knobbly 'Pink Fir Apple', the finest potato of them all, yet famously susceptible to blight. This is the one variety that's worth the trouble. Boiled and dressed as a salad potato it is only surpassed by the leftovers sliced and pushed around a pan with a little garlic and bacon the day after.

Varieties

Potatoes are usually classified by when they are ready to harvest, and by their main use – new or salad potatoes, multipurpose, bakers and mashers.

For earlies: I'd recommend 'Belle de Fontenay' and 'International Kidney' (also known as 'Jersey Royal') for outstanding salad potatoes. 'Pink Duke of York' is a tasty all-rounder that you can dig up early for new potatoes, or grow on larger.

For second earlies: 'Yukon Gold' is excellent for chips, baking and roasting. 'Charlotte' is a reliable and tasty all-rounder and, along with 'Duke of York', well worth considering if you have room for only one or two varieties.

For early maincrop: 'Ratte' is excellent in late summer and early autumn.

For maincrop: 'Pink Fir Apple' is as good as a potato gets.

How to grow

Dig the bed well before planting, but don't add lime. Potatoes love soil that's mildly acidic, and scab will be more of a problem in alkaline soils (see pp.189–90 for more information on soil pH).

'Chitting' is simple but essential. Left in the light in the early spring, the seed potatoes develop nodules (or chits). These are the start of new growth, which while

Harvesting potatoes 'Belle de Fontenay'

desirable, need limiting to focus the growth as you want it. The 'essential' number of nodules is a matter of debate, but two or three chits should see you right. Planting is simple: dig a hole 20cm down (10cm for earlies), place your potato in, chits up, and infill, forming a small mound to help you to spot new shoots coming through. Repeat at 30cm intervals. A handful of wet newspaper or straw plus one of manure in the bottom of each hole is said by some to encourage the potatoes along.

As the leafy tops emerge, tradition holds that you 'earth up' – simply raking up the surrounding soil to create a ridge along the line of potatoes. The idea is to prevent light reaching the top few potatoes, in so doing stopping them from turning green and unpalatable. Earthing up also pretty much takes care of any weeding at the same time. Removing the flowers as they appear is an easy way to increase yield.

How to harvest

Lift early and second earlies as you need them – they'll keep for a week or so only. Allow your maincrop potatoes to dry for a day or two in the sun before storing them somewhere dark in hessian or paper sacks. Whatever happens, ensure you dig up every last scrap of your potatoes each year, to avoid 'volunteer potatoes' the following year, which can harbour blight.

Problems and pests

Your two main problems are likely to be scab and blight (see p.219). The former is a largely cosmetic blotching of the skin – just peel your potatoes. The latter is a fungal disease that can decimate your crop. The best way to deal with blight is to concentrate on early varieties, which are harvested before blight usually attacks.

Blight strikes when it has the heat and moisture it loves, usually in late summer if there is a period of high rainfall. The disease can cause the potatoes to rot (accompanied by one of the worst smells you can imagine), but if you act quickly when you see the telltale dark blotches on the leaves, you can save your harvest. At the first sign, cut all foliage down from any of the infected varieties. With luck you will have caught the disease before it spreads down the stem into the tubers. Leave your potatoes in the ground for 2 or 3 weeks to allow the skins to mature and keep your fingers crossed that when you lift them you'll have your harvest intact.

'Pink Fir Apple' is the one later-maturing variety on which I think it is worth taking the gamble with blight.

How to eat

There's not much you can't do with a potato, as they take happily to just about every cooking method there is. For recipes, see pp.225, 227, 228, 246, 254.

Radishes *Raphanus sativus*

PLANT GROUP	Brassicas (see p.159)
SOW DIRECT	March–September
HARVEST	April–November

Radishes seem to be ubiquitous: if a person has a veg patch, there will most likely be some radishes growing in it. I've always grown radishes, but had the feeling that I was missing a treat when it came to eating them, and then I discovered the reason: imagination. It's not that I don't like the flavour of their peppery roots or their tight crunch – I do, I love it – but there just didn't seem to be much you can do with them, other than bend down and crunch on one when you're wandering past.

Inspired to investigate, I dug out *Jane Grigson's Vegetable Book*. She enthuses passionately about them and mentions a Claudia Roden recipe: thinly slice a few handfuls of radishes, mix with orange slices, dress with orange and lemon juice, add a splash of orange blossom or rose water, plus plenty of chopped coriander. It's amazing. She also tells me that there is a radish festival where they are eaten with brown bread and butter – oh rejoice, I sneer, but on trying it I see why the fuss – it's simple, but delicious. And that's the beauty of the radish. It's worthy of adventurous time spent in the kitchen, yet stands up equally well to a good munch taken fresh from the ground.

Varieties

Radishes come in summer varieties, such as 'French Breakfast' and 'Scarlet Globe', which crop in around a month, as well as the larger-growing autumn/winter varieties sown from late July to early September. If you are growing radishes for the first time, go for a few varieties, sowing them successively (small amounts, every week or two) to ensure a steady supply, and do your own taste test. For winter use: I'd recommend the strongly flavoured 'Rosa'. For summer use: I suggest 'French Breakfast' (long and of medium intensity); 'Pink Beauty' (sweet, round and mild, even when large); and 'Cherry Belle' (crisp, sweet and mild).

How to grow

Sow straight out from March through to September, dotted about in groups or thinly in rows 15cm apart. Botanically in with the roots, in practice you can sow them wherever you like as they're in the ground for such a short time, but avoid areas recently enriched with organic matter as this tends to make radishes split.

Avoid letting your radishes dry out. Steady growth is what they need to avoid splitting or bolting.

How to harvest

There is no quicker-to-harvest food. It only takes a month or so for summer varieties to mature, so a little, sown often, is best. Pick them young and eat straight away.

Problems and pests

Flea beetles may well be drawn to your radishes. Fortunately they usually just pepper the leaves with small holes, leaving the tasty root unaffected.

How to eat

Encouraged by a rather hefty harvest this year, I've found a few more treatments for the supposed humble radish. For Hugh's punchy take on the classic raita: finely slice 200g washed and topped radishes. Mix 300ml natural yoghurt with 100g soft goat's cheese until smooth, then gently fold in the radish and a few chopped mint leaves. This makes a wonderful dip for crudités, and a cool side for spicier food.

For a thrifty, yet tasty soup (also Hugh's), blanch 20 radishes and their leaves with 12 mint leaves in boiling water for a minute, then drain and plunge into cold water. Purée in a blender together with 1 small peeled, cored and diced apple, 250ml vegetable stock (see p.259), 2 tbsp crème fraîche and a pinch each of salt and cayenne pepper, until smooth and creamy. It's delicious warm, but amazing chilled and garnished with a little mint and a few raw radish slices.

For more recipes, see pp.250, 256.

Harvesting radishes 'Scarlet Globe'

Rocket 'Rucola'

Rocket *Rucola coltivata*
and Wild rocket *Diplotaxis tenuifolia*

PLANT GROUP	Salad leaves (see p.166)
SOW DIRECT	March–September
HARVEST	April–November

Rocket – both salad and wild varieties – has livened up the salad bowl no end with its peppery, hazelnutty taste. Both varieties are easy to grow, which is good news considering the price of this salad leaf in the shops. With a little care, rocket will give you a harvest all year round, so make sure you've always got some on the go.

Varieties
Wild rocket and salad rocket are usually sold as generic rather than named varieties. Wild rocket plants tend to be at their best for a little longer than salad rocket, and have leaves that are more incised and slightly milder in flavour.

How to grow
Both types of rocket are happy growing under cover or outside, but will crop slightly more easily under cover in the winter than outside. Sow the seed thinly, direct to your plot any time from early spring to autumn, and harvest either as a cut-and-come-again leaf or pull up the whole plant if you want to use the space. Planting distance is flexible, but 10cm between plants and at least twice that between rows is usual.

Rocket likes to run quickly to seed, so be sure to keep it watered.

How to harvest
Grow rocket for year-round harvesting if you've indoor space for the coldest months. Pick leaves frequently, and at the first signs of toughness, sow replacement plants.

Problems and pests
Flea beetle can be a problem, but damage is usually limited to small holes on the leaves that don't affect the taste.

How to eat
Rocket's peppery hit makes a wonderful addition to mixed salads, yet stands up as a salad on its own – dress with olive oil, a few drops of balsamic vinegar and salt.

Also try it thrown late into a risotto to wilt; as a spiky alternative to basil in pesto; or in place of radish in a soup (see p.121). For more recipes, see pp.238, 242, 248.

Runner beans *Phaseolus coccineus*

PLANT GROUP	Legumes (see p.157)
START UNDER COVER	April–June
PLANT OUT	May–July
SOW DIRECT	April–May
HARVEST	June–October

I doubt there's an allotment in the country without at least one scrambling pyramid of runner beans. They have everything going for them: they're easy to grow, prolific, go on for months, and many varieties put the infamous stringy ones to shame.

If you're already growing your own, you'll need no persuasion to sow them every year. And if you're just starting, then put aside any preconceptions. Just go for a couple of plants though – you'll be amazed at how many beans you get from them.

Varieties
'Polestar' is fantastic – stringless, tasty, and with gorgeous bright-red flowers. 'Kelvedon Marvel' and 'Scarlet Emperor' run closely behind.

How to grow
Sow direct, 5cm deep, when you're confident the last frost has passed, or start them off under cover in root trainers or toilet roll inners (see p.197) in early April, planting them out at a spacing of 25cm a month later. One sowing of a few plants is likely to be plenty as runner beans are prolific – the more you pick the more they produce, pumping out beans for around 3 months. If you don't want to be without them, a July sowing will give you a new supply into the autumn.

Most varieties will easily make 2 metres tall, so they'll need canes or support, either as a tepee or in rows. Applying a mulch will help to retain moisture.

Unlike French beans, which pollinate themselves, runners need to be pollinated by bees, so a few sweet peas or other flowering plants nearby will help to bring them in. Give your plants a warm, sheltered position too, as bees hate the cold and wind.

As with most beans, give them regular watering and comfrey tea (see p.215) from flowering onwards, especially if they're in pots. You can pinch out the tops to get them to bush out below when they reach the height that suits you best.

How to harvest
From June onwards, pick the beans young, small (from 10cm) and often. And pick any larger pods you've missed first time round and try them – continual picking

will ensure your bean factory keeps delivering new pods for longer, and some varieties will still make good eating. When you've had your fill, leave a few pods to grow on – the beans inside swell and are a great butter bean alternative. The flowers are delicious too, but you'll have fewer beans to harvest if you decide to eat them.

Problems and pests

Halo blight (spots with a paler ring around them on the leaves) is usually carried by the seed, so ensure you buy from a good source. Slugs love everything about runner beans, so give this part of your patch particular attention (see p.216).

Blackfly can be an issue. I plant marigolds next to the beans to draw in lots of ladybirds and other insects that feast on these aphids, so I rarely have a significant number. Also, birds may peck off flowers, preferring the red-flowering varieties.

How to eat

I tend to eat almost all of the runner beans I grow either in salads or as a side veg, where they take well to any of the dressings and sauces that work well with brassicas. They're also amazing with a Japanese-style dressing (see p.251).

As the beans get larger, it may be worth peeling off the potentially stringy edges, but there should be no need to do so if they're under 12cm or so.

For more recipes, see pp.223, 256.

Flowering runner beans 'Polestar'

Runner beans 'Scarlet Emperor'

Salsify *Tragapogon porrifolius*
and Scorzonera *Scorzonera hispanica*

PLANT GROUP	Roots (see p.162)
SOW DIRECT	April–May
HARVEST	October–November

Hugely popular in France and Italy, salsify and scorzonera are unquestionably among my desert island veg and I'm shamelessly evangelical about them. They both look a little like a size-zero parsnip, and their flavour, according to fable, is reminiscent of oysters, though I would describe it simply as slightly nutty and sweet. They are also indistinguishable from each other in taste, though not in looks, with salsify paler than its narrower, dark cousin the scorzonera.

If you are hesitant about trying something new, I would urge you to sow half a row of each – partly because both veg are so delicious, and partly to encourage your sense of culinary inquisitiveness. When I first started growing vegetables, I was instinctively averse towards those I hadn't tried before... even more so to ones that I hadn't heard of at all. After all, my logic ran, if they were so good, why were they so little known? Well, this has proved so wrongheaded an approach to food (and maybe even to life) that I have entirely reversed it, taking it as a challenge to find the ways in which any vegetable can be exquisite. Step forward salsify and scorzonera, the first of my vegetable adventures a few years ago, and a fixture in my veg patch ever since.

Varieties
Salsify: 'Mammoth' and 'Giant' are reliable and delicious varieties.
Scorzonera: 'Russian Giant' (also known as 'Black Giant of Russia') is the most widely available variety and the most reliable I've grown.

How to grow
Both veg are pleasingly easy to grow. Sow direct in April or May, 15cm apart, 1cm deep – into soil with few stones that hasn't been manured recently.

You'll need to water the plants during dry periods, but otherwise they will take care of themselves.

How to harvest
They are usually ready to lift in early autumn but can be left in the ground until needed (unless a big freeze is imminent). This is particularly useful if the veg appear

Salsify 'Mammoth' and Scorzonera 'Russian Giant'

small, as their hardiness allows you to grow them on for another year. Simply cut them to ground and earth up in autumn for a chicory-like leaf in spring. These leaves are particularly good to eat, as the local rabbits will attest. Lift the veg very carefully – their roots can be very long and are easily snapped. The flowers are also edible, although not remarkable in my view.

Problems and pests
None.

How to eat
Salsify and scorzonera are delicious braised, baked, boiled or sautéed. It is best to parboil them with the skins on, peeling them after refreshing in cold water.

For an easy side dish to accompany red meat: put the peeled roots into a roasting tin, drizzle with olive oil and scatter with thyme sprigs, then roast in the oven at 200°C/Gas Mark 6 for 20 minutes or so.

My favourite way with either salsify or scorzonera is to enjoy them in a creamy gratin: boil until tender, plunge into cold water, then peel and chop into pieces. Sauté gently in butter, without browning. Tip into a gratin dish and stir in enough double cream to make a sauce without drowning them, plenty of black pepper and a little lemon juice. Sprinkle with parsley and Parmesan and grill until bubbling and lightly browned. Two mouthfuls in you'll resolve to grow them every year.

For more recipes, see pp.225, 233.

Shallots *Allium cepa*

PLANT GROUP	Onions (see p.164)
SOW DIRECT	February–March
HARVEST	July–September

If you're even vaguely short of space but want to grow some onions, then grow shallots (and spring onions) in preference to 'ordinary' white onions. Shallots take up less room on your plot and they're expensive to buy, while you can get maincrop onions cheaply anywhere. If you think that maincrop onions are somehow a larger, better-value harvest due to their size, or you're anticipating fiddly peeling and chopping with their smaller cousins, let me reassure you that shallots are not just small onions. Get ready for a milder yet finer flavour, superior in every way to all the maincrop white onions.

Varieties
'Red Sun' takes some beating as an unusual red shallot, and 'Matador' is a top-notch sweet, yet edgy, shallot.

How to grow
Most shallots can be grown from either seed or mini-onions known as sets. Sets are easier to deal with, but seed is considerably cheaper if you're going for a big harvest.

With seed, sow direct in early spring, thinly in lines 1cm deep and 30cm apart. You're likely to have to thin the seedlings to around 20cm apart.

Plant sets during the first half of the spring with the tips just slightly below the level of the soil. Space sets around 20cm apart, in rows 30cm apart.

Keep your shallots clear of weeds and your crop will enjoy the nutrients it needs. This also ensures good airflow around the bulbs, minimising the risk of disease.

How to harvest
July to September is the time to lift shallots, as their leaves begin to yellow. Let them dry in the sun for a day or two before using immediately, or storing them in net bags for later use.

Problems and pests
Rotating your crops (see p.172) helps to minimise the likelihood of getting onion downy mildew and white rot, though both are comparatively rare. Neck rot can occur during storage. Sort through your harvest well, discarding any that are soft, and use any that are borderline immediately.

How to eat

Shallots can be used in much the same way as maincrop onions in recipes and this is how many people choose to use them. However, I like to save mine for roasting long and slow in their skins to draw out maximum sweetness; for throwing quartered on to pizzas; and for slicing thinly and marinating in red wine vinegar with a pinch of sugar, to add to salads.

If anyone needs convincing that shallots are a bit special, try this way of cooking them: heat a little butter in a large frying pan, add 250g peeled shallots and a couple of rosemary sprigs. As the shallots start to colour, add 2 tsp sugar, followed by a large glass of red wine and 1 tsp balsamic vinegar. Cover and simmer for about 20 minutes. To finish, remove the lid, turn up the heat and let bubble to reduce the liquid until it just forms a colourful glaze on the shallots.

For more recipes, see pp.242, 244, 256.

Shallots 'Matador'

Sorrel *Rumex acetosa*

PLANT GROUP	Salad leaves (see p.166)
SOW DIRECT	March–April
HARVEST	June–November

If you're new to sorrel, it's a perennial that we tend to grow as an annual to keep the leaves from getting tough. Lemony and sharp, sorrel has an acidity reminiscent of rhubarb and gooseberries, yet the leaves are tender, like spinach. They are excellent with oily fish, potatoes, and in soups. And when young and small, you can toss them sparingly into salads. Sow a line and you'll find any number of uses for it.

Varieties
You can gather wild sorrel if you have it nearby, as long as it's not near polluting traffic, but 'Buckler-leaved' and 'Broad-leaved' sorrel are best for your patch.

How to grow
Sow direct in March or April for a steady supply through summer and autumn. Distance between plants is up to you, depending on the size of plant and leaf you are after, but 30cm should do between rows. Water the plants in dry periods to avoid bolting.

How to harvest
Pluck or snip off sorrel leaves regularly for a cut-and-come-again harvest from June until November, or by cutting a few centimetres above the ground to encourage fresh growth.

Problems and pests
None.

How to eat
Don't be put off by the colour change on cooking – from vibrant green to khaki. To prepare, strip out the main veins of larger leaves, then wash the leaves well.

My favourite way to eat sorrel is with new potatoes: cut the prepared sorrel into 1cm strips, toss with the just-cooked potatoes, a little olive oil and butter, then rest for a minute or so until wilted. Season and serve as a side dish or snack on its own.

Sorrel also makes a lovely, punchy soup, combined with a little potato and cream (like a leek and potato soup). And try a few small, young leaves in a salad to pep it up. For more recipes, see pp.223, 246, 248.

Harvested sorrel 'Broad-leaved'

Perpetual spinach seedlings

Spinach *Spinacia oleracea*

PLANT GROUP	Salad leaves (see p.166)
SOW DIRECT	March–October
HARVEST	All year round

Welcome to the incredible shrinking harvest. You'll be sat watching the leaves wilt in the pan and you'll swear you put two dustbinfuls on to cook. Luckily for us, everything that is 'spinach' – the green, the beautifully sharp edge to the flavour – remains after the cooking.

You don't have to cook spinach. It works equally well as a salad leaf when picked small and young, before the leaves begin to thicken. Pick them larger and you'll find they will happily combine with anything from pulses and potatoes to meats. And if you go for the right varieties, you can pick spinach all year round, giving you another versatile leaf to add to your armoury in bridging the so-called 'hungry gap'.

Spinach is also particularly good for you. It's high in both iron and vitamin C, and it just so happens that the vitamin C boosts your body's ability to absorb the precious iron, so you get the maximum benefit.

Varieties

'Dominant' and 'Bordeaux' (F1) are hard to better for autumn and winter leaves, making wonderful salad leaves when picked small. 'Matador' is an excellent variety to try in the summer, as it's slow to bolt – and delicious.

New Zealand spinach (*Tetragonia expansa*) is a must. Although it's not a true spinach, it delivers a similar flavour and importantly grows merrily through the hottest times (even indoors) when many true spinaches tend to bolt. Sow it April–June and watch it sprawl across your patch. You shouldn't need to water it in anything other than drought times, and you can pick the tender leaves frequently when they are just a few centimetres, from mid-summer into the autumn.

Perpetual spinach (*Beta vulgaris* var. *cicla*) (see p.60) is unrelated but gives you similar(ish) leaves seemingly endlessly. It's well worth sowing a few to ensure a year-round factory of versatile leaves.

How to grow

Sow direct once a month from March through to early autumn (depending on your varieties) for a year-round crop. Any variety can be sown early in spring and early autumn, but try Matador for June–August sowings. Go for rows about 30cm apart, and try to sprinkle thinly – 3cm or so apart. Thin to 20cm if you are after large leaves. If you are picking small leaves as a cut-and-come-again crop, you should get a harvest in little over a month in optimum conditions, perhaps twice as long when it's cooler. Watering is vital to steady growth of the plants and it minimises the likelihood of bolting – little and often is ideal.

How to harvest
Keep cutting leaves, when they are around 3cm or so above ground level, to encourage more growth.

Problems and pests
Apart from the stage when spinach is at its most vulnerable to slugs as it emerges, it is rarely troubled by any pests or diseases.

How to eat
Pick spinach small and it's a fantastic addition to most leafy salads, but as soon as the leaves are medium-sized, they will have lost their succulence and are better cooked. Spinach makes a lovely partnership wilted with chick peas or potatoes, taking perfectly happily to the milder end of the curry spices.

Hugh's creamed spinach is particularly good: strip the stalks from 500g spinach and wash the leaves well. Cook with only the water clinging to the leaves from washing in a covered large saucepan until just wilted. Refresh briefly with cold water, drain well and squeeze with your hands to extract as much water as you can, then chop roughly. Put 250ml milk in a pan with a sliced onion and 2 bay leaves. Bring almost to the boil, take off the heat and leave to infuse for 10 minutes, then strain into a jug, discarding the onion and bay. Melt 50g unsalted butter in the pan and stir in 25g plain flour to make a loose roux. Cook gently for a couple of minutes, then stir in half the warm, infused milk. Cook, stirring, until the sauce is thick and smooth, then incorporate the rest of the milk. Bring to the boil and simmer gently for a minute. Season well with salt, pepper and a generous grating of nutmeg. Next, stir in the chopped spinach. Heat through, but don't let it bubble for more than a minute. Taste and adjust the seasoning with salt, pepper, and a touch more nutmeg perhaps. Serve at once, ladled into large warm bowls. Simple, yet delicious, and if you're in the mood, a little Gruyère or Parmesan grated over the top works a treat.

Or for a tasty snack, wilt 500g spinach, refresh, dry and chop as for creamed spinach (above). Beat 2 eggs with a little Parmesan, a good grating of nutmeg and a good pinch each of salt and pepper. Add the spinach and just enough breadcrumbs to hold the mix together fairly stiffly, then shape into squash-ball-sized nuggets. Heat a good glug of olive oil in a frying pan until just smoking, and fry the nuggets for 5 minutes or so until golden all over. Let them cool a little, then serve warm rather than blisteringly hot, with a punchy (garlicky or mustardy) mayonnaise.

For more recipes, see pp.223, 244, 248.

Spring onions *Allium cepa*

PLANT GROUP	Onions (see p.164)
SOW DIRECT	October–November for overwintering varieties; or February–August
HARVEST	February–November

As soon as I munched through a 'White Lisbon' I was hooked, and everything from salads to tarts to mashed potato to cold meats gets the mild punch of spring onions now. On top of that incredible flavour, they're easy to grow, and take up next to no room to generate all that flavour. Treat them as a salad, but also get used to them as one of those multi-purpose transformers that add to – and make more of – so many of your other harvests.

They work wonders for some of your plants in the garden as well as the kitchen, acting as an ideal companion plant (see p.212) for carrots, with their oniony smell disguising the carrot scent that would otherwise attract the damaging carrot fly.

Varieties
'North Holland Blood Red' looks and tastes the best of the spring onions, although 'White Lisbon' isn't far behind. 'White Lisbon Winter Hardy' is the best for overwintering to get an early crop.

How to grow
Sow them thinly direct into your patch in lines around 10cm apart, thinning (and eating) them as they grow. Give them a sunny, well-drained spot. Sowing them in small amounts every few weeks from the end of February until the start of August will give you a steady supply into autumn. Winter-hardy varieties sown in October and November will give you an early harvest, starting around Valentine's Day.

As for routine care, a little careful weeding (avoiding the shallow roots) is all they'll ask of you.

How to harvest
With a range of varieties successively sown, you can have spring onions from February right through to November. Pull them up as you need them, using the thinnings as you go.

Problems and pests
Onion downy mildew and white rot are rare and incurable, but if you avoid growing onions in the same place 2 years in a row, you're unlikely to get either.

How to eat

Sliced thinly, spring onions bring punch and crunch to any salad, and they take well to the griddle or barbecue. I particularly love them sliced as thinly as possible in salad dressings. If you've any mashed potatoes left from a meal, then throw in chopped spring onions along with any leftover chopped greens, and shape the mix into cakes for shallow frying as the classic bubble and squeak.

For more recipes, see pp.226, 239, 244.

Spring onions 'White Lisbon'

Sprouting broccoli

Brassica oleracea var. *italica*

PLANT GROUP	Brassicas (see p.159)
START UNDER COVER	March–April
PLANT OUT	June–July
SOW DIRECT	April–May
HARVEST	January–April

The 'hungry gap' at the back end of winter and early spring can feel like the garden's annual holiday. It's certainly a lean time compared to summer, but what is around can be truly special. Step forward sprouting broccoli. Admittedly, when there's little to harvest, there can be a temptation to overhype the average, but these flavoursome spears make it a true veg patch essential. It comes in either white or purple varieties, which not only help fill the hungry gap, but almost make you glad there's little else about so you can concentrate on getting your teeth stuck into them.

I'm not sure how sprouting broccoli has managed to remain a relative secret, given that it is one of the very, very finest foods your garden can produce. I suspect it may be a triumph of the supermarkets. Sprouting broccoli has a delicate, complex flavour and is more tender than calabrese. It's also comparatively short-lived and tricky to pick in large quantities – all of which points the supermarkets towards calabrese. They've managed to divert our attention with ease, with calabrese not only winning the race to our shelves over sprouting broccoli, but even managing to pinch its name on the way.

Varieties

Sprouting broccoli is available in a range of varieties that produce at slightly different times, allowing you to stretch this delicious harvest over a longer period. For earlies, try 'Rudolph' and 'White Eye'; for mid-season, I'd recommend 'Red Arrow'; for lates, 'Claret', 'Late Purple Sprouting' and 'White Star' are all good choices. You could even try one of the new summer-cropping varieties, such as 'Bordeaux', but there's something about sprouting broccoli in the heat of full summer that doesn't seem quite right to me – I prefer to enjoy it in its season.

How to grow

Start them off under cover in Jiffy 7s (see p.197) or small pots in March/April, planting out when they are around 10cm tall in June or early July. Give them 50cm between plants. Alternatively, sow direct in April/May.

Sprouting broccoli 'Purple Sprouting'

Make sure you water your sprouting broccoli plants if there's a dry period in the first few of months after you've planted them, but don't water them through winter – they'll do fine on their own.

Problems and pests
Slugs and snails are the main threat. Patrol regularly and deal with them in whichever way you prefer (see p.216).

How to harvest
Sprouting broccoli is a cut-and-come-again veg, and if you choose the right varieties, you can help yourself from New Year through to April. As with most cut-and-come-agains, regular harvesting pays dividends, prompting the plant to keep on throwing out tasty arms, so make sure you get out there with the basket every few evenings. Slice off entire shoots when they're young and tender – and certainly before they risk going to seed as this halts production.

How to eat
In the finest of edible baton-passing, the sprouting broccoli starts to dip off just as the asparagus kicks in, and you can treat them exactly the same: steam the spears quickly before dipping in hollandaise or dressing with good olive oil, lemon juice and freshly grated Parmesan.

If you find yourself with too much on your hands (an impossibility surely), then blanch in boiling water for a couple of minutes only, drain, cool quickly in cold water and freeze in batches.

For more recipes, see pp.233, 244, 258.

Squash, pumpkins and gourds
Cucurbita maxima, C. pepo and *C. moschata*

PLANT GROUP	Cucurbits (see p.165)
START UNDER COVER	March–May
PLANT OUT	June–July
HARVEST	October–November

This threesome comes in almost any shape and colour imaginable and there's little to touch them for spectacular productivity. If you're a first-timer, try a few as they'll reward you on every front – they're very hard to mess up, they look incredible, they swamp out the weeds locally, and not only do they pump out a sizeable harvest, they also keep well, allowing you to enjoy them long afterwards.

The distinction between pumpkins, squash and gourds is bizarrely vague, and even their botanical names provide little guidance. If it helps, I tend to think that pumpkins are generally orange, gourds are mostly inedible, squash are almost always delicious. So, concentrate on squash for the kitchen, a pumpkin or two for Hallowe'en, and decorative gourds to weird up your plot.

Varieties
There is such a variety of delicious and peculiarly shaped squash available that you can try a new cultivar every year if you like, but there are three you should start off with: the creamy and versatile 'Early Butternut' is a real must, as is 'Crown Prince' (F1), which looks, tastes and stores as good as any, and the onion-shaped 'Red Kuri' (aka 'Uchi Kuri') with its deliciously sweet, nutty flesh. Other possibilities are 'Jaspée de Vendée', a heavy cropper with a delicate flavour, and the flatter 'Tancheese' with its slightly sweeter salmon-coloured flesh. If you're after an outstanding edible pumpkin, look no further than 'Rouge Vif d'Etampes'. For Hallowe'en, 'Atlantic Giant' is perfect as it lives up to its name impressively.

How to grow
Start them off under cover in spring in small pots or Jiffy 7s (see p.197), sowing each seed on its edge to prevent rotting. When they have reached a good size with four leaves or so and you're sure the frosts have passed, plant them out at least a metre apart – the leaves will fill up the sea between them, keeping weeds out and soil moisture in. Dig a good-sized scoop and fill the hole with compost, planting your seedling in and watering well. Squash and pumpkins will repay any investment in richness and moisture at this stage.

Squash 'Red Kuri'

How to harvest

Don't be too impatient when it comes to picking pumpkins and squash – leave them to ripen as long as you can. If the weather turns wet for more than a few days, slip a roof tile or something similar under them to prevent them from sitting in the damp. Ready or not, when the frosts approach it's time to cut them. Pick them with a short stalk, as this seems to ensure against (most) rotting in storage. Place them somewhere light but not too warm – they'll continue to ripen a little for a week or two longer. Most will store well into the winter.

It isn't advisable to save seed from squash or pumpkins. Any cross-pollination that may have occurred will come through in the next generation, leading to unpredictable taste.

Problems and pests

Slugs and snails are a threat for a few weeks after planting out, so you'll need to keep these in check (see p.216).

How to eat

Squash and pumpkins roast so well you'll probably find that's the first port of call for much of your harvest. Don't bother with peeling them first, just slice them up chunkily, scrape the pips and fibres out and toss then in a roasting tin with a splash of olive oil, a good sprinkling of sea salt and black pepper, and a few garlic cloves. Roast in a preheated oven at 200°C/Gas Mark 6 for half an hour or so until tender, turning them at least once.

To make a tasty soup, roast a reasonable-sized pumpkin or squash as above, then cut away the skin and peel the garlic. Using a blender, purée the roasted squash or pumpkin flesh with the garlic and 1 litre vegetable stock (see p.259), in batches if necessary. Return to the pan and warm through gently. Thin with a little extra stock (or milk) to the desired consistency, check the seasoning and serve scattered with thin strips of crispy bacon.

Don't discard the seeds from your pumpkin or squash, as they're both delicious and highly nutritious. Wash and dry them, then spread out on a roasting tray, scatter with flaky sea salt and roast in a hot oven at 200°C/Gas Mark 6 for a few minutes to bring out the flavour.

Both squash and pumpkin also work well finely diced and gently cooked in olive oil with a little garlic. Use as a risotto base (outstanding with a little rosemary), or – with the addition of a little vegetable stock and/or cream – as a pasta sauce.

For more recipes, see pp.248, 254, 262.

Swede *Brassica napus* var. *napobrassica*

PLANT GROUP	Brassicas (see p.159)
SOW DIRECT	April–June
HARVEST	September–February

This is very possibly the least glamorous vegetable of them all. It has rivals (notably the turnip) but swede has the edge, I think. With its rough, matt skin and tendency to become fibrous when allowed to grow too large, swede offers little in the way of initial culinary promise, yet it is a really valuable addition to your veg patch. The secret is to focus on its qualities and keep it simple. Although we think of it as a root veg, swede is a member of the brassica family, and therefore botanically in with the cabbages and broccoli. So as well as harvesting the deliciously sweet root, have confidence that the leaves are not just there for photosynthesising – these are top-notch greens for the table.

Famously popular in Scotland, swede is an essential element of Burn's Night celebrations, when it is traditionally served with haggis. South of the border swede was, until recently, the pre-pumpkin vegetable hollowed out and carved with faces to make Hallowe'en lanterns. Ugly maybe, delicious double-croppers certainly, good for you definitely, and you can carve a novelty face out of them: what more could you want from a vegetable?

Varieties
'Willemsburger' has a green top rather than the usual purple one, producing good-sized roots with pale orange flesh of excellent quality. It's also resistant to club root (the main disease you might encounter), and keeps well, so even if you try other varieties, give this one a go too.

How to grow
Sow swede direct from April–June, thinning the emerging seedlings to at least 20cm apart.

Keep the plants well weeded to minimise competition. Water them through dry periods, but note that a steady amount for a few days is better than a lot in one go, as they'll happily split if there are serious fluctuations in water supply.

Problems and pests
Slugs may damage the leaves and tops of swedes as they emerge, which can lead to rotting from the top. Make sure you include your swedes as part of your regular slug patrol (see p.216).

How to harvest

Lift swedes throughout the autumn and winter, twisting off their leafy tops. If you find you have a surplus, store them in a wooden box of moist sand.

How to eat

Treat the tops as cut-and-come-again leaves, picking half and leaving the rest for the plant. The cabbage pasta sauce treatment (see p.45) works wonderfully well with swede tops – a little chilli in the mix is particularly fine.

The skin is quite thick and uneven, so when preparing, first quarter the swede and then peel with a knife rather than a vegetable peeler. Roasted or mashed, swede is a wondrous, sweet accompaniment to roast meat, game and poultry. Just bear in mind that roasting or steaming concentrates the flavour, whereas boiling dilutes it. Drain swede thoroughly before mashing and don't be shy with butter, cream and freshly ground black pepper.

For more recipes, see pp.225, 253.

Swede 'Willemsburger'

Sweetcorn *Zea mays*

PLANT GROUP	Others (see p.169)
START UNDER COVER	April
PLANT OUT	May–June
SOW DIRECT	May
HARVEST	July–September

Sweetcorn is the ideal crop for beginners and even more so for children as it grows quickly, vertically and obviously, communicating the wonder of growth and life as well as any vegetable there is. And on top of that, of course, you get to look forward to popcorn.

If you intend to eat the cobs fresh rather than as popcorn, remember that they're right up with asparagus and peas when it comes to minimising plot-to-pot time. As their name implies, it's the sweetness you're after. In this respect, every hour counts, as the sugars quickly convert to starches after the corn leaves the plant – eat them on the day you pick them if you can.

When it comes to cooking, it's worth knowing that sweetcorn is one of those rare crops that, if overcooked, is in fact better for you. Although their vitamin C quickly reduces, the levels of ferulic acid shoot right up with long cooking at high temperature. Why is this a big deal? Ferulic acid is an antioxidant – one of those great caretakers of our internal system running about sweeping up potentially damaging free radicals that can contribute to physical changes we perceive as ageing, as well as heart disease and cancer. Most ferulic acid is held in the cell walls and fibres within the sweetcorn and cooking breaks these down, liberating the bioactive bodyguards to go about their rather wonderful business. So, for once, you can boil the backside out of this veg with impunity.

Varieties

A lot of the newer varieties are known as 'supersweet', having higher levels of sugars – 'Sweet Nugget' (F1) and 'Sweetie' are the best I've tried.

It is well worth giving some of the older varieties a whirl too. Many prefer what they feel is a better balance of sweetness with the sweetcorn's other flavours – 'Golden Bantam' is reliable and tasty. Be sure to check whether the seeds you are buying are supersweet or normal, as you'll need to allow significantly more room if you grow some of each (see page 147).

If you (or your children) are after popcorn, 'Strawberry Sweetcorn' is hard to beat and a beautiful ornamental addition to the veg patch.

Sweetcorn 'Golden Bantam'

How to grow

April is the best time to get sweetcorn started under cover in pots or Jiffy 7s (see p.197), planting them out when around 7cm tall and the frosts are definitely past (around May or June).

Leave it until May if you're sowing sweetcorn direct. Plant the seeds knuckle deep, with spacing 30cm each way.

Sweetcorn are wind pollinated (unlike most other vegetables which are pollinated by insects). It's therefore better to plant them in groups rather than rows if you can, to maximise pollination. You should allow at least 8 metres between supersweet and normal varieties, as cross-pollination may reduce their sweetness. The plants grow well if there is a reasonable blend of rain and sun, giving you a harvest from mid-summer into autumn.

Water them well after flowering if there's an extended dry period.

How to harvest

By early summer (depending on variety) the flowers will have appeared at the top of the plant, puffing out clouds of pollen that can turn you, the soil and hopefully the tassels on the plant yellow. Each of these untidy tassels is actually a thin tube connecting the outside world with a grain, patiently waiting to be fertilised. If you're lucky, the pollen hits its target, and in a few short weeks you'll be munching the results. The cobs are ready when the tassels turn dark brown. Stick a thumbnail into one of the niblets, and if the liquid released is milky, your sweetcorn is ready for the pan; if it's clear, then leave it a while.

After picking, if you can't eat your sweetcorn immediately, keep the leaves on as this helps retain freshness, and get them in the fridge quickly to slow the conversion of sugar to starch.

Problems and pests

None.

How to eat

You can mess around with sweetcorn to your heart's content, adding it to any number of salads, but little beats boiling and eating them simply with butter, salt and pepper. (Don't salt the cooking water though or it will harden the kernels.)

Or you might like to try barbecuing them, leaves on – the slight burnt flavour combines well with their sweetness, and gives you another opportunity to use any leftover confit chilli (see p.230).

For more recipes, see pp.242, 248.

Tomatoes 'Costuluto Fiorentino'

Tomatoes *Lycopersicon esculentum*

PLANT GROUP	Solanaceae (see p.168)
START UNDER COVER	February–March
PLANT OUT	April–June
HARVEST	July–October

A tomato at its best, wrapped in a basil leaf, is summer in a succulent globe. Warm from the sun, your first home-grown 'Gardener's Delight' is likely to be up there with any harvest you grow, but if you want to ripen it to its perfect peak, it pays to know a little about the deceptively complex tomato. There's a fine line between reaching this peak and overdoing the physical compromise that comes with it. As the flavour develops, the tomato becomes softer, more prone to damage – and judging that is half the fun of growing them. Erring on the cautious side, supermarkets focus on getting them intact from soil to shelf, so their tomatoes are picked early and firm, never attaining the flavour of vine-ripe tomatoes and often bland.

Yet a home-grown crop can sometimes be little better, or utterly delicious, or anywhere in between. Why such uncertainty when other foods that ripen, bananas, say, are pretty much the same every time? With around 400 sugars, acids and volatiles contributing to the mix, tomatoes are just that much more complex. With so many variables, it's not hard to see how we can get anything from a tinny trebly tune to a bassy bottom-heavy boom.

And that's not all. Not only are there endless permutations when it comes to these compounds, but they are far from stable within the tomato itself. The colour change from green to red isn't just a change of wallpaper, it indicates a deeper chemical transition within. The acid balance moves from appley malic acid towards the sharper citric acid, with the sugars shifting from glucose to the far sweeter fructose. Added to this, the volatiles are jumping about too. And then there's our easily fooled senses – the sharper citric acid makes the sweeter fructose seem even sweeter to us, as does the change to a softer texture. So ripening, it seems, is far from a linear process: every last tweak of chemical ripening can multiply itself in terms of our experience of it.

But the tomato is no soup of sugars, acids and volatiles washing about willy-nilly – it holds many of these compounds separately in its structure, and the act of slicing, chewing or heating breaks down the constraining boundaries, causing enzymes to hit compounds, sweetness to touch acid, flesh to merge with juice, giving us a tomatoey jumble of jostling flavours. Ripening involves essentially the same breakdown and intermingling, increasing towards the peak, which contributes much to our enjoyment of that elusive hit of whole, perfect tomatoeyness.

It's good to understand why the tomato can be anything from delightful to disappointing, but more importantly it hints at why it can be so tricky to get to the tomato we are after. So, safe in the knowledge that it's not your fault if your tomatoes turn out so-so, relax, and enjoy giving them a go. What you must do is prepare well, choose a range of good varieties, and keep the plants fed and watered (as outlined below). You'll still need an element of luck, though, to get all those sugars, acids and volatiles to line up just so. But as with the old adage, the more you practise the luckier you'll get – there's simply no short cut to getting to know which tomatoes do best on your patch. Talk to your dad, your neighbour, the oldest allotmenter you can find and ask what works for them, as they may have some great ideas. And trust yourself too – developing a little touch and a knack is all about trying things out and watching and encouraging a little luck to come your way.

Varieties

Tomatoes are particularly sensitive to place, so try at least four varieties to start off with and stick with the ones that thrive, trying a few more each year.

Unless you've a compelling reason to do otherwise, it's well worth trying each of the different types: 'Gardener's Delight' is rightfully the ubiquitous cherry, although 'Orange Bourgain' makes an excellent alternative; 'San Marzano' is a flavoursome plum; of the extra-large tomatoes, 'Costuluto Fiorentino' and 'Brandywine' are outstanding and reliable, with 'Burpees Delicious' living up to its billing.

Of the yellow tomatoes, look no further than 'Sungold' – it's deliciously sweet. 'Tumbling Tom' is the one to try for growing in hanging baskets. 'Black Krim' is another variety worth growing, not only for its remarkable red-black skin, but for its firm yet juicy texture and incredible flavour – perfect for tomato salads and salsas.

If you're going for some outdoor tomatoes, plump for varieties that ripen early – they may just give you the edge you need to get a mature crop, as they'll need less sun. Most cherry tomatoes should give you a good chance.

How to grow

Start tomatoes off under cover in February or March in Jiffy 7s (see p.197) or modules. When they get their first true leaves (following the initial pair of 'seed' leaves), move each plant into a 10cm pot, planting them 5mm below the height of the seed leaves.

Plant them out when they reach around 20cm tall, with flowers starting to open on the lowest truss. A sheltered, sunny spot is vital, as is a good, fertile medium in which to grow, so incorporate well-rotted manure and/or compost a couple of months ahead of planting them if possible.

Your plants will need a little support – canes for tying the taller cordon varieties (single-stemmed plants, occasionally sold as 'indeterminate' varieties) to, or netting and/or a few shorter sticks for bush varieties (also known as 'determinate' varieties).

The key to success is simple – tomatoes want sun, water and feeding, so make sure they get them. Tomatoes have one set of roots at the surface for feeding and other deeper roots for drinking, so bear this in mind when caring for them. You can bury a piece of pipe or an upturned plastic bottle with its base cut off next to the plant and use it to get the water down to where it counts. This isn't essential, but there are those who swear that surface watering dilutes flavour. After flowering, the fruit will start to set and a good drenching once a week with comfrey tea (see p.215) or seaweed feed will make all the difference. Remember that 'little and often' is the mantra – split fruit is all you'll get for drought followed by overwatering.

Shoots that develop between the stems and the main leaves must be removed as they use up valuable nutrients and water that your fruit needs, increase shading and reduce air circulation. Simply pinch them off. Cutting off the top of outdoor plants when six trusses have set fruit is usually advised to focus energies on the fruit, and most people do this on indoor plants too. Another thing I tend to do is pull off some leaves as the fruit ripens to promote air and light access, and so reduce the chance of disease. It's a balancing act between leaving plenty of leaves for the plant to photosynthesise but still getting the sun and air around your fruit.

How to harvest
The indoor harvesting stretches from July to early autumn, but outside you may be waiting into September for it to kick off. For that reason alone I prefer to grow most indoors. Any unripe outdoor fruit can be picked in the second half of September and ripened on a sunny sill – the ethylene given off by a nearby banana can shunt the process along, though they won't quite match up to those turned by sun alone.

Problems and pests
Companion planting works wonders with tomatoes. Garlic and nasturtiums repel aphids with their smell, whereas basil draws the aphids to it and away from your prize crop for you to deal with as you like (see p.212).

Tomatoes can suffer from the same blight as potatoes (see p.219), so avoid planting any outside if yours show any signs of the disease. Growing them under cover (as I do) will much reduce your chances of getting blight, but do make sure you don't grow them in the same spot year after year in your polytunnel or greenhouse to avoid the risk of disease building up in the soil.

How to eat
Tomatoes have an affinity with many ingredients – basil of course, but also cheeses, olives and anchovies – offering delectable salads and endless other culinary treats. Cold dramatically affects their flavour, causing an irreversible decline in the aromatics especially, so don't refrigerate! For more recipes, see pp.230, 256, 259.

Turnips *Brassica rapa*

PLANT GROUP	Brassicas (see p.159)
SOW DIRECT	March–July
HARVEST	June–October

I grow turnips every year for the pigs to nose through in autumn, but this year I allowed them (the turnips that is) to cross the line between field and garden, and I'm glad I did. With their sweet, peppery roots and outstanding leafy tops (spicy, like mustard greens) they have been one of this year's garden surprises. A couple of varieties disappointed, but this is to be expected, as turnips are famously unreliable in taste. Any variety can be delicious on one patch, bland on another, so try a few, and persevere with the winners.

It may be that as a nation we have been alone in missing out on a classic double harvest. As I write on the first weekend in November, I discover that I am but one tantilising Saturday shy of the annual turnip festival held on the banks of Lake Zurich in Switzerland. Apparently this is Europe's largest turnip festival, the rather scary implication being that there are other rival turnip festivals out there desirous of our attendance. Web-searching confirms how widespread these root raves are, and how almost unique we are in consigning the turnip to livestock fodder.

Varieties
As turnips vary in performance depending on location, recommending particular varieties is tricky. Try three or four and see which do best in your conditions. For me, 'Atlantic', 'Snowball' and 'Purple Top Milan' have come out tops.

How to grow
Sow direct in a shady spot every 3 weeks from late March to July, although be aware that early sowings can tend to bolt. Thin gradually until the plants are at least 15cm apart, using the discarded thinnings as greens.

You can also keep sowing (with no need for thinning) through August and September for delicious cut-and-come-again green tops to harvest in early spring.

Keep the plants watered through dry periods, but keep the watering consistent as fluctuations may cause them to split.

How to harvest
Pick your turnips when the roots are no bigger than a snooker ball, ideally smaller, through summer and autumn if you've sown successionally. Late-summer sowings (or early autumn under cover) will give you delicious leafy greens in March.

Problems and pests

Don't be fooled by your eyes, turnips are brassicas not roots, and they can suffer from the same ailments as most of the others. Club root is best avoided by rotating where you grow your plant groups each year (see p.159). Flea beetle may well leave its trademark peppering of tiny holes in the leaves, but they shouldn't be more than a passing nuisance.

How to eat

I do think we can learn a trick from the French and Swiss who braise or sauté turnips. They are also delicious roasted in a little honey, or try them – as the Italians favour – in risotto. They also make a deliciously different 'risotto' of their own, taking the place of the rice itself (see p.247). And turnips are surprisingly good when sharing the main duties with potatoes in the dauphinoise recipe (see p.254).

Turnip tops are one of the finest greens you'll eat – they'll take well to anything from a simple steaming to a spicier treatment. Try them with the pasta sauce that works so well for cabbages (see p.45).

For more recipes, see pp.225, 253.

Turnips 'Purple Top Milan'

Plant Groups

Almost all the food on your wish list falls readily into one of the main plant groups – legumes, brassicas, roots, onions, cucurbits, salad leaves, Solanaceae and perennials. The rest I've thrown into a catch-all group I've called 'Others'. It's worth looking through the next few pages and familiarising yourself with what each of these groups gives and takes from your veg patch, as they will be key to guiding you on how you organise your plot. Check out the tips for growing each group successfully too. Remember, time invested now pays dividends all through the rest of the year.

Legumes

Borlotti beans	see p.36
Broad beans	see p.39
French beans	see p.79
Peas	see p.110
Runner beans	see p.124

If you've got better things to do at 8 o'clock on a mid-June evening than pop freshly shelled peas into your mouth as you amble around your vibrant plot with a glass of what you fancy, then life must be pretty special.

Peas and beans are packed with protein, they're cheap and easy to grow, and many arrive early in the growing year to encapsulate the taste of spring and welcome in the warmer days. They also come with the almost unbelievable bonus that they nourish the garden as well as the gardener. Nodules in the roots convert nitrogen from the air into compounds that feed the plant as it grows. When the plant dies or the top is cut off, the nitrogen is released into the soil as the roots break down, naturally fertilising your patch for subsequent plants. So plant legumes in spring and miraculously that bed will be more fertile in autumn.

With many of the legumes, every minute between plot and pot counts towards retaining their sweetness, so growing your own is really the only way to get to enjoy them at their sweet succulent prime. Having said that, the more I grow, the fewer seem to make it to the kitchen. Caught young and small, so many of them make delicious fast food as you wander about your patch.

Peas and beans are best started off under cover, planting out when they've reached several centimetres tall. Mice and birds love to tuck into seeds, so if you sow direct be prepared to lose a few, especially from autumn and early spring sowings.

Grow legumes in a well-drained plot to get them at their best, and remember to give them their rightful place in your crop rotation (see p.172), as this minimises the likelihood of disease. Pea and bean weevil can be a pain, producing the stamp-edge notches you'll see in leaves, but they rarely get beyond nuisance status. It's the slugs and snails that are your main enemy. Hit them early and hit them hard – go out every other night at dusk, disposing of any you find.

As well as the edible legumes, you're likely to come across a few others that are grown with the purpose of benefiting the soil. Known as green manures, most do as their edible cousins do and leave the soil enriched with nitrogen, so it pays to get familiar with how they can help bump up your harvests (see p.208).

In growing legumes you're not only feeding yourself and your soil, you may also be doing something for the planet. I can think of few things that better illustrate the wrongheadedness of our food supply than green beans and peas topping the list of the most air-imported fruit and veg – above exotics such as grapes and pineapples.

Growing legumes in small spaces

All of the legumes will grow happily in containers, although (like those grown outdoors) most will be grateful for any support you can give them. Canes and twigs can be tied into supporting tepees (see p.211), and with the help of a little netting or wire mesh, the climbing legumes will happily crawl up walls, taking up very little of your ground space.

Don't let containers dry out, and do give them a weekly watering of comfrey tea (see p.215) from flowering time onwards.

Tips for success with legumes

• Sow successionally
• Start them off under cover in root trainers or toilet roll inners (see p.197)
• Plant them where you grew potatoes last year
• Give them a sunny site
• Many climb, so do give them a sheltered spot
• Remember to give them support or grow dwarf varieties
• Pinch out the tops to encourage lower, bushier growth
• Water with comfrey tea once a week after flowering to encourage maximum pod production

Brassicas

All stemming from a wild original species, the brassicas provide an exhibition of natural and professional selection at its most varied. Coloured purple, white, black, green, red, yellow, blue – and everything in between – they offer the cook an array of edible roots, stems, flowers and leaves, yet we usually lump them together as 'greens'. They are generally regarded as narrow variations on a theme, though the reverse is true. How many of us even clock that we are eating flowers when we tuck into our calabrese, sprouting broccoli or cauliflower?

Not only do they offer diversity for the kitchen, many are stunning. Choose the right varieties and grow them at their happiest time of the year and the brassicas can deliver something delicious for the table every week of the year – beautiful and productive, the perfect combination.

You'll need to spend a little time getting to know the brassicas as varieties are particularly idiosyncratic – happy on one plot, poor on the next. Try a few of each and persevere with your favourites, dropping the others for new trials. It's worth the effort. With most brassicas, you won't notice a difference if they hit the plate a minute rather than an hour after picking, but grow the right varieties well and you'll appreciate their home-grown flavour is far superior to any in the supermarkets.

As with any plant group, a few rules will guide you to success. Although brassicas germinate well if sown direct, slugs, snails and birds will be rubbing their imaginary hands with glee as the leaves poke up. So start them off under cover in pots, modules or Jiffy 7s (see p.197), planting out when there's at least four leaves on the plant.

If you need convincing about rotation (see p.172), let the prospect of club root clarify your mind. The disease infects the roots, creating cysts which impair the flow of nutrients to the upper parts of the plant. Your crop will be poor at best, but worst still, the disease persists. Once you have it, you are stuck with it. There is no cure.

Cabbage 'January King'

The best way to tackle it is prevention – and rotation helps ensure that there is less risk of build-up. Sowing your own brassicas (rather than buying in seedlings) also helps to ensure they are free from the disease.

Cabbage root fly can be a nuisance, attacking brassicas when they're vulnerable after planting out. If you want to be preventative, put a flat cardboard collar around the stem to block the flies getting to the join with the soil to lay eggs. Interplanting with pungent herbs also helps to confuse those pests that navigate by smell. Hand-pick caterpillars (mostly cabbage whites) that show up in the sunnier months. I prefer this to netting, which usually works but detracts visually and impedes access.

Flea beetle can be a pain to most brassicas, but they particularly target radishes – nibbling small holes in their leaves that cumulatively impair the plant's ability to photosynthesise. Tolerance is usually the only alternative to chemical remedy, or you could try the ever-inventive Bob Flowerdew's remedy (see p.218).

Growing brassicas in small spaces

Brassicas are the plant group that takes least well to growing in containers. Their typically long growing time from sowing to harvest not only takes up space to the exclusion of quicker harvests, it often exhausts the nutrients found available in a confined space. Most won't die but your chances of getting a top-quality harvest are limited by your dedication in feeding them.

Given how strikingly beautiful many brassicas are, you may be better to use them in any garden space you have, to add extra appeal to your flower beds.

Tips for success with brassicas

- Club root loves acid conditions, so neutralise your soil pH with lime if you need to (see p.190)
- Never grow them in the same place within 3 years
- Grow them where legumes grew last year to benefit from the residual nitrogen in the soil
- Incorporate organic manure well ahead of planting
- Start them off under cover
- Try a number of varieties of each and persist with the ones that work best on your veg patch
- Plant in firm ground (and/or tread in well after planting) to ensure anchorage
- Give each plant some room, brassicas like air circulation
- If possible, give them a shady site rather than full sun
- Go out on regular slug, snail and caterpillar patrol – it will really up your harvest

Roots

Beetroot	see p.33
Carrots	see p.50
Celeriac	see p.56
Celery	see p.58
Parsnips	see p.108
Salsify	see p.126
Scorzonera	see p.126

With the early-summer sweetness of baby carrots, the autumnal earthiness of parsnips and the wintery possibilities of celeriac, I doubt there's another food group to touch root veg for year-round variety. Yet they have a rich history of under-appreciation and are subject to inconsistent prejudices. Roots may have seen many through wartime scarcity, but several European countries seem to have had their fill and their particular staple has lost its appeal: the French love a turnip, but not a parsnip. Then there's mistrust of the unknown: in England few savour salsify, while in Italy it is worshipped. Every root is revered and reviled with seemingly equal enthusiasm.

Roots may not be helped by their looks, but don't judge this book by its less-than-glamorous cover – their typically rough, thickish skin is precisely what we should be grateful for. It protects the body of the root and retains water, allowing us to store them until we need them. The root itself is the energy store full of sugars (providing immediate energy for the plant) and starches (its long-term reserves) and it is this wonderful combination we prize for its sweetness and fine texture. We also owe a debt to the defence system of some roots. It prompts the starches to quickly convert to more sugars should the plant feel under threat – hence parsnips taste sweeter after a frost. Some even produce sulphurous compounds to ward off attack, which we taste as the mustardy hit behind radishes and horseradish.

The key to giving roots the prominence they deserve in your patch is to focus on variety. Most of us eat our fair share of potatoes, onions and carrots, but we can readily source them locally. Cutting back on maincrops of each will free up some of the precious plot to try lesser-known, yet tasty roots like salsify and scorzonera.

You'll need patience and a little trust to grow roots. There's not the usual visual encouragement, nor a moment's stolen grazing: it's all going on, but mostly unseen. As a rule, roots are unfussy and most of your work comes before planting – in ensuring a good deep tilth for uninhibited growth. Avoid adding compost to the soil, as this encourages most roots to fork. You're after steady, deep-rooting growth, which allows the plant to draw up and accumulate minerals as a tasty prize.

For culinary perfection, size is often critical. The world of sport offers the best guide to prime harvests – golf and snooker balls for the best beetroot, baseballs for celeriac. But in truth, optimum size (and therefore spacing) is pretty flexible, and should reflect how you like to eat them. Close spacing gives a larger harvest of smaller veg, and vice versa. For what it's worth, I prefer small to medium root veg in the warmer months, slightly larger ones as the weather gets colder.

Growing roots in small spaces

Many of the roots will do well in containers of at least 25cm diameter and depth. If you want larger specimens of any roots, a stack of three tyres filled with compost is perfect, but you'll need to keep them well watered. Even if you're not short of room, this is an excellent way of getting an early crop of summer carrots under cover.

Tips for success with roots

• Prepare a good deep, fine bed
• Only add compost as a top dressing
• Think of roots as year-round harvests rather than just winter warmers
• Space closely for smaller crops (mainly in the warmer months), and further apart for larger veg
• Don't let them dry out, especially those closely planted, as they will have a greater tendency to bolt, becoming woody to eat. Remove any that do immediately, as they are thought to release chemicals that induce their neighbours to follow suit.

Onions

Garlic	see p.81
Leeks	see p.97
Onions	see p.102
Shallots	see p.128
Spring onions	see p.135

The onion family is right up there in that group of culinary transformers, taking many of your other harvests to a higher place in the kitchen. Stew without onions, vichyssoise without leeks – both unthinkable. From sharpness and crunch, through to soft, sweet and mellow tastes, family members have different qualities to offer. They also stand up on their own with the right treatment – typically long slow roasting to refocus the flavours and bring their natural sweetness to the fore.

Happily most members of the onion family are pretty easy to grow, and if you rotate your veg beds you should have little trouble from diseases. That said, this is one area of your patch that you can look to rationalise if you're stuck for space. Most maincrop onions are cheaply available and of pretty high quality in the shops. In most cases these maincroppers are not the home-grown flavour revelation that, say, peas are. So unless you have a real desire to grow all your onions, and have plenty of space to do it in, consider dropping at least some maincroppers for shallots, red onions, spring onions and a few garlic varieties – the real gastronomic treats.

Growing onions in small spaces
Spring onions are perfect for containers, trays, and even small spaces between other plants in the ground. Similarly, if you've only a small patch of ground I'd recommend growing even a few heads of garlic, as they make a beautiful addition to any garden.

Tips for success with the onion family
- Grow them together with roots as part of your 4-year rotation (see p.173)
- Use some of the smaller members of the onion family as companions with carrots to deter carrot fly
- Concentrate on growing shallots and other more unusual and expensive members of the onion family
- Sow into warm soil to reduce the tendency to bolt
- Give them a sunny open site for best results – they need good air circulation to discourage diseases
- Keep them well weeded – they hate competition

Cucurbits

Courgettes	see p.67
Cucumbers and gherkins	see p.69
Squash, pumpkins and gourds	see p.140

If you're either a novice, or lazy or have little time, cucurbits should come right near the top of your wish list as a delicious, varied easy-to-grow lot. All you need to make the cucurbits happy is a moist rich soil to grow them in, a sunny spot and a willingness to water at the first sign of dryness. If your soil needs enriching, add well-rotted manure and/or compost before planting.

Such is their apparent desire to reach your table, your main difficulty may well be in avoiding an over abundant crop. Known (at least in my house) as cucurbiquity, the result is squash, cucumbers and courgettes (especially) seemingly everywhere. The best advice to avoid your harvest becoming more of a hassle than a joy is: not to plant too many; to have a handful of fantastic recipes ready for the inevitable surplus; and to pick your courgettes, cucumbers and gherkins small and frequently. This will give you maximum flavour to minimum volume, and avoid that 'not again' feeling when they do rather better than you had envisaged.

If you are after the ideal place to grow them (or are short of room) any of the cucurbits will grow very happily in your compost heap, drawing on the rich nutrients therein, and getting a gentle nudge from the heat of the decomposition process.

Growing cucurbits in small spaces
Cucurbits are rambling space takers, but with the right varieties you can train that growth vertically over canes, netting, arches, or indeed anything you might like to hide in your garden. Check the catalogue description for squash, cucumber, courgettes and gherkins that are happy to scramble.

Most of the cucurbits will do well in containers, though you will need to make sure these are large enough. You'll also have to water them well and give them the occasional feed once they start to develop fruit.

Tips for success with cucurbits
• Start them off under cover
• Give them room to grow
• Water them regularly
• Harvest courgettes, cucumbers and gherkins small and frequently
• Mulch them early on to help retain water (see p.210) – the leaves should do this for you as they grow

Salad leaves

Chicory	see p.62
Endive	see p.74
Lettuces	see p.99
Rocket	see p.123
Sorrel	see p.130
Spinach	see p.133

For years, I couldn't see the point of eating something that didn't even provide me with enough calories to finish eating it, but now that I've come to concentrate on the range of salad leaves I can grow, rather than just hearting lettuces, my attitude has changed. As I write, I have lettuce leaves of 'Marvel of Four Seasons' and 'Green Oak Leaf', the bitterness of chicory and endive leaves, peppery wild rocket, the lemony sharpness of sorrel, along with pea tips, endless herbs and edible flowers, as well as a few oriental leaves to choose from. I'm after a salad with a variety of flavours, textures and colours, and my plot now reflects this.

Focusing on leaves has been the single largest revolution in my veg patch. Gone is the waste that usually comes with too many lettuces hearting all at once, and I get deliciously different salads every time.

Most salad leaves are packed full of antioxidants – those mysterious beneficials that appear to help the body to deal with all manner of ills. But there's little point in getting your daily dose from bags of ready-washed supermarket leaves. Apart from all that packaging, the likelihood is they've been 'washed' in a chlorine solution. The positive side of supermarket salad bags is that they've given many of us a taste for eating mixed leaves, and the seed suppliers have been quick to catch on.

The variety of leaves available to grow is vast compared to even a few years ago. There's the crunchy, the floppy and the multi-coloured, the peppery, the lobed, the mustardy, the crinkly, the bitter. And salad leaves are just as much of a taste sensation in the winter as the summer. With a little forethought, you can have their crunch, punch and goodness right through the winter, as well as through the warmer months. Happily, they are easy to grow, pretty forgiving of site, need little more than the odd watering, and many will grow again if you take a harvest of leaves. Added to that, salad bags are expensive to buy, so you've every reason to grow them.

The very notion of salad is also becoming increasingly and deliciously blurred. Many of the leaves traditionally grown for cooking are finding their way (usually picked small and tender) into salads. Spinach, chard, some kales, oriental leaves, edible flowers, pea tips and herbs all add to your salad-making choices. You can even turn salads into delicious main courses with the addition of meat, fish, seeds, nuts and cheese. The possibilities are further multiplied if you experiment with interesting dressings. So, if like me you've been a bit indifferent when it comes to salad, it's time to elevate them above the 'good for you' part of the plate. Give them their own stage, afford them at the very least some good oil and some sea salt. You'll be amazed.

Growing salad leaves in small spaces

This is the easiest of all the plant groups to grow in small spaces. Most are quick to mature, take up little room and will give you leaves from any container. To save time and space, sow leaves for cutting rather than hearting. Try leaves for repeated cutting in guttering, seed trays or in pots on your windowsill.

Tips for success with salad leaves

• Most can be sown direct, but all do better started in modules or in guttering
• Unless noted for a particular variety, don't let the soil dry out or the plant will feel stressed and run to seed
• Weed little and often
• Regular slug and snail patrols will greatly increase your harvest
• Cut or pick leaves a couple of centimetres above the soil and your plant will resprout a number of times before they tire

Solanaceae

Aubergines	see p.31
Chilli peppers	see p.65
Peppers	see p.114
Potatoes	see p.117
Tomatoes	see p.149

The potato shares its family with a rather unlikely crew of Mediterranean favourites – the aubergines, peppers, chillies and tomatoes. In theory, this means that they should share the same bed. In practice, all but the potatoes tend to be grown in a polytunnel, greenhouse, in a growbag or in a pot.

If you're feeling optimistic and are trying any of the sun lovers outside, then it's sensible to start them off under cover and plant them out where you've just lifted your earliest potatoes. If any of your potatoes have blight, then grow your tomatoes indoors or in a container as they are susceptible to the disease too.

Growing Solanaceae in small spaces

A stack of three tyres filled with compost is the perfect growing medium for a crop of early indoor new potatoes whether you've a shortage of space or not. Tomatoes, aubergines, chillies and sweet peppers are just about ideal for small spaces.

You might construe having no room outside, or only concrete next to the house, as possible limitations, but it needn't be the case with these sun lovers. It simply means that you'll end up growing them either on a sunny windowsill, or on a balcony, or in pots or a growbag against a wall – all of which will give them the light, heat and shelter they'll love.

Keep the plants well fed with comfrey tea (see p.215) from flowering onwards to ensure they have the nutrients required for fruiting.

Perennials

Asparagus	see p.28
Cardoons	see p.48
Globe artichokes	see p.85
Jerusalem artichokes	see p.92

Most of the inhabitants of your veg patch are annuals – germinating, maturing and being eaten within a year – but there are also a few absolutely prize long-livers that every patch should have. This group is the edible equivalent of the self-refilling pint: plant them once and almost unbelievably you'll be in for harvest after harvest, year after year. Each is easy to establish, fairly low maintenance, top of the flavour charts and expensive in the shops – the perfect qualifications for growing your own.

You can plant the perennials anywhere you like, but life is likely to be simpler if you give them a bed (or beds) of their own.

Others

Chard and perpetual spinach	see p.60
Edible flowers	see p.72
Florence fennel	see p.76
Herbs	see p.87
Oriental leaves	see p.105
Sweetcorn	see p.145

The rest fall into a catch-all group I've called 'others'. This disparate bunch is either outside the main plant groups or in the case of oriental leaves (many of which are brassicas) do not need to be grown with the rest of their family. Plant them where you like around your veg patch.

Planning your Veg Patch

Every mid-November when the fire's working hard and

I feel the need for the beer to be kept out of the fridge rather than in it, I know it's time to look through seed catalogues. Part of me knows it's a bit ridiculous to love this time so much, but what I read now is what I'll be eating in a few short months and I can't help but get hungry at the prospect. It's a menu of sorts, it's just that the service takes a little longer.

You may not be drenched in mid-summer sweat or digging up the plot in early winter, but as you stretch out in front of the flames with a glass in one hand and a catalogue in the other, the work you are doing is every bit as important as the graft at any other time of the year.

As well as choosing and ordering varieties, this is the time to organise your plot a little, and to do that you'll need to know a little about plant rotation.

Planning your rotation

If you're looking for an easy life as well as the Good Life, you'll need to start thinking early about how you want to organise your patch. To do that you'll need to understand the principle of plant rotation – the fundamental process that will minimise pests and diseases and maximise your harvests.

The idea of plant rotation couldn't be simpler: most of your plants will do better if you grow them together in their plant groups and if you don't grow them in the same place each year. There are a number of reasons for this.

Plants from the same group:
- Tend to enjoy the same conditions – growing them together makes it easier to provide them with this
- Often grow and mature at similar times – grouping them makes it easier to clear larger areas and prepare for the next crop
- Are often planted/sown at similar times, making most effective use of prepared ground and ensuring that bare earth is minimised
- Are usually susceptible to the same diseases – grouping them together and moving them each year helps minimise the risk of diseases building up
- Often have specific nutrient requirements – growing them together helps provide this, while rotating helps ensure that the soil doesn't become depleted

There are endless ways of planning your rotation but at River Cottage we use the simplest: the 4-year cycle – it's easy to split your patch into four, and to my mind the plant groups fall most naturally into this rotation plan. Start with this and you'll not go far wrong.

The beds for a 4-year rotation

THE LEGUMES BED

Where we put all the legumes – broad beans, beans, peas, etc. Notable for the ability of the roots of these plants to take nitrogen from the air and make it available in the soil for other plants.

THE BRASSICA BED

For all the brassicas, such as broccoli, cabbages and kale. This bed also includes a couple of those oddities that we think of as roots, but that are botanically brassicas, notably turnips and swede.

THE ROOTS AND ONIONS BED

Although separate families in their own right, these two are often grouped together for the purposes of the veg patch. The root family includes many of our underground tasties – carrots, celeriac, parsnips, etc. As well as onions themselves, the onion family includes garlic, leeks and shallots.

THE POTATO BED

Potatoes, although gastronomically treated as root vegetables, are in fact tubers and usually given a bed of their own. They belong to the Solanaceae family, which also takes in aubergines, peppers and tomatoes – all of which, if you grow them outside, can go in this bed.

Each of these four beds influences its part of the plot in specific ways, with its own associated diseases and nutrient needs. To ensure that this pattern of giving and receiving is balanced and that diseases are not given the opportunity to build up, the beds are moved around the garden in rotation.

Following our system, rotation involves splitting the heart of your patch into four sections and keeping a very particular order to the rotation. Where you grow legumes this year you should grow brassicas next, roots and onions the year after, potatoes in year 4, and then back to legumes.

The order is important for many reasons, most notably to ensure that the plants which produce nitrogen in the soil (the legumes) are followed by plants that benefit most from more nitrogen in the soil (the brassicas).

	Year 1	Year 2	Year 3	Year 4
Plot 1	LEGUMES	BRASSICAS	ROOTS & ONIONS	POTATOES
Plot 2	BRASSICAS	ROOTS & ONIONS	POTATOES	LEGUMES
Plot 3	ROOTS & ONIONS	POTATOES	LEGUMES	BRASSICAS
Plot 4	POTATOES	LEGUMES	BRASSICAS	ROOTS & ONIONS

As mentioned earlier, perennials – asparagus, artichokes, the perennial herbs, etc – are best given a permanent home out of the main rotation. Cucurbits, annual herbs, salad leaves and the 'others' can be happily slotted into your plot anywhere you like.

Making a paper plan

The more you do indoors, the less you'll run into trouble later outside. Get some graph paper (or print some from a web source) to help plan out your plot. But before you think about plants, consider your infrastructure: where's the water coming from, where do you want your main paths and where will you put the compost bin?

Water
Alongside the health of the soil and the amount of sunlight, the availability of water is the major influence on the success of your crops, but you'd be amazed how many aspiring growers convince themselves that they can happily haul a couple of watering cans back and forth from a distant tap: don't make that mistake.

If you've any way of harvesting rain water then take it, and leave yourself outside the grasp of any hosepipe ban. Shed and greenhouse roofs have a surprisingly large surface area and guttering secured to them can direct much of the water you'll need to a storage tank. Water butts are invaluable (check with your local council, many have offers for them), as are at least two watering cans. If you have water on tap, invest in a long and durable hose, and a reel for it.

Paths and access
In your eagerness to get as much out of your patch as possible, don't overlook the need to get to your plants regularly as they're growing – a plateful of tomatoes loses something of its reward when you've tripped over the squash, become tangled in the borlottis and flattened the basil in the process. Give yourself room to get about.

For your paths, work out the breadth you think you need to get yourself and a wheelbarrow around, then widen them by another 30cm. Believe me, a few well-placed narrow paths amongst your beds won't be enough.

Compost bin

This is the ultimate recycling centre – you'll turn to this stack of nutrients regularly to enrich your soil, and in turn care for your plants. There are a number of options to choose from, including making your own compost bin (see p.203), but whichever you take, don't be tempted to put it too near your veg. Snails and slugs love breeding in compost and will happily make short journeys at night to eat anything close by.

The beds

Once you've taken care of water supply, main access paths and where the compost is going, you'll need to define your beds and what you plan to grow in them. If you're looking to grow your veg in four main beds plus one or two for perennial plants, then I'd recommend you consider the perennial bed first. Decide how much you want to grow and determine its size from that. Then split what remains of your plot into quarters, allowing for more paths to give you access to them.

The key measurement when mapping out your beds is your reach. Don't have beds that you can't comfortably reach the middle of, otherwise sooner or later, you'll tread on your precious soil, compacting it in the process: 1.5 metres is an ideal width for beds, if you have access from all sides. If for any reason you want a wider bed than you can reach to the middle of, source a few wooden planks to walk on, as this spreads your weight and compacts the soil much less. Old scaffold boards are ideal.

Keep referring back to the patch itself, and ask yourself if your paper plan feels right looking at it on the ground. Amend it as you go. Take every opportunity to look at other plots, and take advice from neighbouring allotmenters. All can help you get to the design that best suits you and what you're growing.

Tips for your paper plan

• Measure your patch and use graph paper to help you draft out a plan
• Give yourself plenty of room for paths and easy access
• Visit open gardens and allotments, and stare over hedges for inspiration
• As your plants may need extra water, plan for where your supply will come from
• Site your compost bin away from your main beds
• Remember, your reach is most important – don't plan to grow more than you are confident of coping with, and make sure that you can reach all of it from your paths (or planks)
• If your space is more than you need, you can always grow into it – use green manures (see p.208) or cover unused areas with durable mulch mat (see p.210)

Growing seasonally and successionally

Now that you've organised your plot spatially, your concern is what happens over the course of the year. To get the most from your plot, you'll need to plan not only what goes in to start with, but also what follows. You'll need to think successionally. This is more straightforward than it might at first appear. All the information you need to help you plan when to sow and when you're likely to harvest each food is to be found in the A–Z. Successional thinking is about paying as much attention to the harvest time as to the initial sowing, and getting seedlings ready to take the place of crops as they finish. So when you're drawing up a plan for where you'll be growing your veg, write down next to each when it is harvested, and it will become second nature to ask yourself questions such as 'When the potatoes come up, what goes in?'

You'll also want to ensure that you don't have great gluts of one food all at once. When it comes to your plot 'little and often' is usually best, and this goes as much for your harvests as any other part of growing your own. Apart from the food that keeps for months (such as parsnips and squash), you should aim for a slow supply to match your consumption. This becomes increasingly important the shorter the shelf life of each harvest. Salad leaves, radishes and summer carrots are quick to go past their best, so a glut inevitably means wastage.

To combat this, you have two main strategies, Firstly, sow at intervals to ensure your harvest comes gradually. Secondly, sow your seeds under different conditions (some indoors, some under glass, some outside) and they'll reach maturity at different times. A good tip: as you go to plant out any seedlings you've started under cover, sow a fresh batch. That way you'll always have seedlings following on behind.

With year-round availability in supermarkets, seasonal produce has rather taken a back seat. There can be some strange comfort in buying pretty much the same food every week, but having any food any time you want it comes at a price. The eating calendar necessarily uncouples from the growing year, losing its subtlety. You may be able to buy asparagus on bonfire night, but it'll be a pale imitation of the real thing, and have been flown halfway around the world. It also robs asparagus of that dimension that comes with it and many other foods: anticipation.

If you're taking the step to grow your own food then try not to supplement your harvest with too much imported veg. Give yourself a chance to appreciate the wonder of each season and what it brings to your plate. If you celebrate your harvests as they come, your home-grown menu will never tire – there'll always be a new crop around the corner. Little can match the heavenly baton-passing of purple sprouting broccoli to asparagus and on to peas, except perhaps the anticipation of it. To be out of step with the rhythm of the seasons is to assume that tomatoes are somehow 'better' than parsnips, or that summer is superior to winter – and when you're in step every flavour is something to relish in its place in the seasonal swing.

Common garden considerations

A veg patch works best when gardener and garden are in harmony, so it pays to spend a little time being sensitive to the limitations and opportunities provided by both. The balance between ambition and practicality is a tough one to strike, and if you have to make a choice I'd urge you to come down on the side of practicality – better to make a success of something smaller than be overwhelmed.

Be realistic about the shortcomings as well as the opportunities of your plot. If you stare cold-eyed at what you have, the chances are you'll make the best of it and turn as many of the seemingly negative aspects to your advantage as is possible. Make a list of what's good and bad, and ask your partner or a friend to check it over – we aspiring gardeners can be beautifully blinkered in our enthusiasm! You may have one or two of the following common garden 'shortcomings', but don't worry, they are far from insuperable.

Limited space

The classic. What you have never seems enough – if you have a balcony you want a courtyard, if you've a courtyard you want a garden, if you've a garden then gimme a field. Everyone has limited space as far as they are concerned. In truth, no matter what size of patch, we can all grow more on it than we think we can, and whether you've a tiny garden, an urban courtyard, or a high-rise windowsill you can still claim your share of the harvest.

The secret lies in making the most of what you have, taking innovation and integration to the max, and searching out new and space-saving ways of growing your food.

One of the best ways of squeezing a harvest out of a small area is to grow your plants in containers. Pots, small raised beds, hanging baskets and planters all allow you to tailor your growing area to suit where you are. You'll need to keep a more vigilant eye on watering, replace the compost in pots every year, and perhaps offer the occasional comfrey feed (see p.215) to keep the nutrients topped up. Be inventive and look for recycling and reusing opportunities, such as colanders, large food cans and ceramic sinks – anything with drainage. This year I grew potatoes in tyres, and carrots in leaky wellies that would otherwise have been thrown out. They were both prolific and delicious.

Even a square metre patch on the ground extends skywards for as high as you like: use it. Supported by canes, tepees, netting or wires, many tall growers will give you a substantial harvest while taking up only a minimal footprint on the ground. And don't forget 'vertical' doesn't just mean upwards – balconies and hanging baskets provide the perfect base from which to grow dangling crops like tomatoes ('Tumbling Tom' is a great cascading variety) and strawberries.

Growing veg in small spaces

		SMALL BED	POTS	TYRE STACK	WINDOWSILL
LEGUMES	Broad beans	●	●		
	Borlotti beans	●	●		
	French beans	●	●		
	Peas	●	●		
	Runner beans	●	●		
BRASSICAS	Brussels sprouts	○	○		
	Cabbages	○	○		
	Calabrese	○	○		
	Cauliflower	○	○		
	Kale	○	○		
	Radishes	●	●		●
	Sprouting broccoli	○	○		
	Swede	○	○		
	Turnips	○	○		
ROOTS	Beetroot	●	●	●	
	Carrots	●	●	●	
	Celeriac	○	○		
	Celery	○	○		
	Parsnips	●	●	●	
	Salsify	○	○	○	
	Scorzonera	○	○	○	
ONIONS	Garlic	○	○		
	Leeks	○	○		
	Leeks (baby)	●	●		●
	Onions	○	○		
	Shallots	○	○		
	Spring onions	●	●		●

		SMALL BED	POTS	TYRE STACK	WINDOWSILL
CUCURBITS	Courgettes	o	●	o	
	Cucumbers and gherkins	o	●	o	
	Squash and pumpkins	o	●	o	
SALAD LEAVES	Chicory	●	●		●
	Endive	●	●		●
	Lettuces	●	●		●
	Rocket and wild rocket	●	●		●
	Sorrel	●	●		●
	Spinach	●	●		●
SOLANACEAE	Aubergines	●	●		●
	Chilli peppers	●	●		●
	Peppers	●	●		●
	Potatoes	o	●	●	
	Tomatoes	●	●		●
PERENNIAL	Asparagus	●	o		
	Cardoons	●	o		
	Globe artichokes	●	●		
	Jerusalem artichokes	●	●	●	
OTHERS	Chard and perpetual spinach	●	●		
	Edible flowers	●	●		
	Florence fennel	●	●		
	Herbs	●	●		●
	Oriental leaves	●	●		●
	Sweetcorn	●	●		

● = recommended
o = feasible

Look for inventive ways of growing plants together. A traditional way of growing in a small space, known as the Three Sisters, allows you to grow a climbing legume, sweetcorn and a cucurbit together in mutually supporting harmony. The climber will feed the other two with its nitrogen-fixing roots while taking advantage of the sweetcorn for scaffolding, while the cucurbit (such as squash or courgette) crowds weeds out, keeps water in and cools the roots of all three. You may also find you have chances to snatch a quick crop from alongside your main harvest. If you sow salad leaves, radishes and other fast-maturing crops alongside a chilli plant in a pot for example, they will reach picking time before the chilli needs all the space in the pot.

If you have a small garden, you might wonder whether you can free up any space for vegetables. Even if you are attached to the loveliness of the flowers, you may find that the ornamentals you grow can give you something for the table too. Globe and Jerusalem artichokes, purple cabbages, fennel, giant red mustard, nasturtiums and chives are all attractive inhabitants of a border that will give you a delicious harvest.

It also pays to match up your conditions with your plants. If you've a small garden with a warm wall, get the sun lovers next to it to benefit from its extra heat, and consider painting it white to bounce those rays around even more. If you've a cool, shady or north-facing wall, get the plants which like it out of direct sun there, and consider training a morello cherry against it. You can even introduce a mini greenhouse into your small space by investing in a cloche (shown below), building a cold frame (a short, glass-lidded box), or using plastic water bottles with the bottom cut off to bring the benefits of extra heat and frost protection to your patch.

Lettuce under a cloche

You should also consider bringing the outside inside. Windowsills and porches can make your house the engine room for your plot. Great places to start seedlings off, they are also ideal for taking many plants through to harvest. As well as pots and other containers, you can keep guttering or seed trays on windowsills filled with cut-and-come-again salad leaves, giving you a continual harvest from a small space.

The secret to growing your own in a limited space is to be positive and creative. If you look hard enough, there'll be a way to grow at least some of your own food.

Extreme soil conditions

Soil pH can range anywhere from strongly acidic to strongly alkaline, and texture varies from sand to clay, with the ideal for growing most plants being somewhere in the middle of both. If you find yourself out at either end, don't worry, there is much you can do to nudge yourself towards the centre of the spectrum (see p.189).

An exposed site

While a little breeze is desirable to help air circulate, strong winds can severely limit the success of your crops. If you find yourself at their mercy more than occasionally, then I'd urge you to put up a fence at the outset. Fences, hazel or willow hurdles, or the usual array of hedging shrubs will all do the job, but if you're after a return from your boundary, consider making it edible. Many of our hedgerows offer up a seasonal harvest – of crab apples, cherries, elderberries, sloes, plums, hawthorns and more. Perhaps include something different, such as cherry plum or bay. Italian alder grows quickly with the added bonus of feeding your plot with its nitrogen-rich leaves as they fall, or get the best of both worlds with the autumn olive (*Elaeagnus umbellata*), which not only grows rapidly, it also fixes nitrogen (see p.212) and gives you lovely fruit for jam. Plant what suits your patch and your taste buds. Anything but leylandii.

A sloping site

If your patch is on a steep incline, you may think the pinnacle of your troubles is in getting your wheelbarrow from the bottom to the top, but the likelihood is that a slower, less visible process is your main enemy. As it rains, your precious soil will begin to wash away, running off with the downpour and taking with it not only your most valuable resource, but denying it the full benefit of the water soaking in.

The solution is terracing. The idea is simple – divide your slope into as few level patches as you can and as many as you need to make the steps between them practicable. It can be a tough task, and if you ask me, this is where a driver with a digger is a good investment – they'll have it done in no time. Short hedges across the slope also work wonders to arrest the downhill slip of soil, but your prime concern is to always keep the soil covered – if not with edible crops, then with green manures (see p.208) as this greatly reduces erosion.

Common gardener considerations

Never mind the soil, the climate or the aspect – your key consideration is what *you* can and can't do when it comes to dedicating time with your hands in the earth. Time, money and access are the big three limitations as far as the gardener is concerned, but these need not be obstacles, merely realities to accommodate. The soundest advice, as before, is not to bite off more than you can chew.

Starting up is all about anticipation and planning, carrying on is all about confidence and momentum. The most essential ingredient is to make sure your time in the veg patch is something you enjoy. Don't let it become a bind or chore.

Limited time

Chances are you'll not be short of competing calls for the time you'd like to spend on the plot. You'll want to get there twice as often, you'll want to stay there twice as long when you do. But do try to dedicate a little time as often as possible, rather than make lengthy but infrequent visits – and be realistic about your time commitment from the start. Match that to your plan and your reach will meet your grasp.

Creativity is your saviour when it comes to limited time. There's *always* a way of doing something smarter. Try integrating some of the high-maintenance harvests with your life rather than relying on you going to them. Keep the needy crops where you spend more of your time, whether it's outside the back door, on a windowsill, or in the office. Keep much-munched herbs in pots near the kitchen, and go for cut-and-come-again leaves on your balcony and windowsills. Let your plot come to you.

The less time you'll have to tend your plot, the more important your initial preparation is. The quality of your infrastructure becomes even more crucial, as you don't want to spend all your precious evening hauling water from a distant pipe to seedlings, nor re-edging your paths as they seek to recolonise your once-pristine beds. If time is tight then take a day's holiday in the winter before you even think about planting, to create paths that don't grow: you'll never have to spend time stopping a concrete slab encroaching on your lettuces. Keep everything simple.

Limited money

Having a veg patch will involve more than a few beans changing hands, especially in the start-up year. There are many ways of keeping costs to a minimum, and which works best depends on what you can offer.

Money is not the only exchangeable resource – time, surplus harvest, skills and machinery are the classic smallholder's currency, equally acceptable to many gardeners. Swap, sell, exchange in any way you can think of – part of the harvest in exchange for the seeds to sow it, a morning's weeding for some seed potatoes, a few hours' loan of a rotovator for help laying a path.

Seeds are often inexpensive, but if you're short on cash, planning a larger plot or are after some of the more expensive varieties the price can add up considerably. Bear in mind that your first year is likely to be the most expensive. In subsequent years you can save seed, use the remainder of the first year's and exchange some of what you have left for new varieties. To get off to an affordable start in year one, talk to friends, neighbours and fellow allotmenters. Many will have some seeds left from the previous year and be happy to barter them for a slice of the harvest.

Organised seed swaps are also becoming much more common again. If you haven't already, get used to the idea of shoeboxes and drawers full of half-empty seed packets that to everyone else are half full. That is just about the best definition of the conditions that create a market as you can get. All you have to do is link the owners of all those shoeboxes, and the best way to do that is to join a group, either physical or virtual. Sign up to local horticultural societies or try allotment groups, pin a notice up at work, tell everyone you know.

And don't forget to sign up to the River Cottage Community (see p.266). Run independently, it relies on the combined experience of thousands of members, and that's an awful lot of virtual garden fences to peak over. There's an organised seed swap every year, along with a lively Farmers' Market section for selling or requesting anything at all to do with bringing your own food to the family table.

If you're looking to turn a profit, you may be up against it, but those who are time-rich and well schooled in the art of preserving and household thrift might, just might, make growing food a sensible economic exercise. Factoring in the costs of alternative ways of getting the benefits you glean from your plot (such as going to the gym) certainly helps balance the books, but in all probability your reward will be more to do with health, happiness, and the genuinely life-enhancing pleasures that come with eating rather than feeding.

Limited access

Many aspiring growers find their nearest allotment is at the other side of town, which can limit ease of access. The issues thrown up often equate to limited time, and many of the ways of alleviating them also apply. Going for low-maintenance plants, investing in preparation and avoiding grass patches that need mowing and edging are all sensible routes to take. It's also vital to keep your seedlings where you spend more of your time – this is the stage of their lives when they need most frequent attention, so use those windowsills, balconies and porches.

On-site storage can make all the difference too, and although these may be at greater risk due to infrequent time spent at your plot, having your tools on site can make a real difference if your main mode of transport is anything other than a car. Get yourself a shed or a lock-up container (a galvanised feed bin does fine) to keep your most used tools in.

Creating your
Veg Patch

Gardeners tend to fall into two groups: those who put the majority of their energies into looking after the plants, and those who concentrate on the ground they grow in. Belong to the second group. Your primary job is to care for the soil, and it will (for the most part) look after the plants. Remember, however much of a slight it may be to your ego, it's not you that grows the plants, it's the soil – so treat it as a close friend.

I make no apologies for repeating the importance of planning: the growing year magnifies what you do well and what you do less well. Get it right and life on the plot will feel incrementally rewarding, take short cuts and you'll find you're paying for it exponentially as the ramifications compound. Every second spent bending your back in January on preparation saves a minute on your knees in April when you're busy sowing, and rewards you with an extra hour on your backside enjoying your harvest at its height. So it pays to be a little patient early on. Hold back the urge to get planting and spend a little time investing.

Clearing

The closer you can get to starting with a weed-free patch, the better. If your plot is a jungle of perennial weeds (such as ground elder, bindweed and creeping thistle), the ideal approach is to dig up any large brambles and cover the ground with a light-excluding mulch for at least a year to kill them off. Digging and ongoing weeding will only engage you in an endless wrestling match, rotovating will only multiply the enemy. The likelihood is that your plot is a step or two back from this jungle, and if so, there's little else for it but to acquaint your palms with the handle of a fork.

If you can, dig over your plot in late autumn or early winter, as this will allow a long period for the weather to break down the clods into something approaching the tilth you're aiming for. Some growers will tell you to double-dig your veg patch, which involves digging down to twice the depth of your spade's blade. I favour a minimum-dig approach, disturbing the soil structure only when essential. So, I'd recommend you dig only to the depth you have to, in order to clear the plot.

Dig up any perennial weeds like docks, roots and all, and either burn them or tie them up in a bin bag to decompose fully before incorporating them into your compost. Any annual weeds can be composted, although if you're in any doubt about what's annual and what's perennial, throw it in with the perennials to be safe. If you think you have many annual seeds in there (if it's an allotment that's been used for a while, chances are there will be), cover the plot with clear plastic for a fortnight to encourage them to germinate quickly, then hoe them off.

There are alternatives to the traditional dig-it-all-clear method, notably the no-dig approach whereby beds are created above the existing soil surface (see p.193).

Getting to know your soil

It's a good idea to learn to love your soil right from the off. You and your plants will be relying on it for sustenance and if you understand a little about its character you'll form a much stronger partnership with it. The two qualities you'll need to familiarise yourself with are soil texture and soil pH, both of which will play a large part in influencing the health of your plants... and therefore the quality of your suppers.

You can tell a lot from your soil by how it feels (see soil texture, below) but if you really want to get inside it, a professional soil analysis is undoubtedly the most thorough way to go. It's simple: send off a few trowelfuls to a soil analyst and they'll tell you about its texture and its pH (see p.189). See the directory (p.266), for those offering this service. With a professional analysis, you will also learn a little about the nutrient balance within your soil. Don't be too daunted by this: it can be interesting to uncover more about the wonderful stuff that nurtures your plants. In truth, however, if you keep adding organic matter – ideally in the form of your own compost – you'll right any significant imbalances naturally.

If you prefer the DIY approach you can also get good basic information from a few simple tests that you can carry out for yourself (see below and p.190).

Soil texture

The main mineral components of soil are clay, silt and sand. Sand particles are the largest, followed by silt, with clay particles the finest. Soils with a lot of sand are free-draining, whereas those comprised of predominantly clay particles are water-retentive and lie at the other end of the soil spectrum. It's no surprise that a reasonably equal mix of each – namely, a loamy soil – is what you're after.

The perfect loam blesses few of us. Thankfully there is much we can do to nudge things towards the happy medium, but to get there we need to know where our soil is starting from. Almost all soils will fall into one of the groups described overleaf. There are soil types outside these groups, but they are rare. In such cases, the area is unlikely to be used for cultivation (thin moorland soils, for instance) or will be famously productive (some fen soils, for example). If this applies to you, you're best to seek professional advice specific to your location.

You can do a rough-and-ready texture test yourself. Take a little of your soil, the size of a golf ball, and squeeze it gently together in your hands. If you need to, add water, a little at a time – you want just enough – until you get a putty-like consistency. Keep kneading and squeezing until you have broken any clumps down. Try to make it into a ball: if it won't hold together you have a sandy soil. If it has formed a ball, try to roll it to form a worm: if it won't you have a sandy loam (i.e. between a loam and sandy soil); if it forms a worm up to 3cm long you have a loam; a 3–6cm worm indicates a clay loam, and a longer one suggests a clay soil.

Testing soil texture

Loamy soils Loams are the gloriously desirable average, a middle ground derived from reasonably equal amounts of sand, silt and clay. These soils enjoy something of the good-draining qualities of the sand, balanced with some moisture-retaining capabilities from the clay and have good levels of nutrient availability. If you are lucky enough to have one of these soils, rejoice.

Sandy soils These freely draining soils are easy to work for most of the year and have much going for them, notably that they warm up very quickly in spring. However, their easy drainage can be a problem: the large particle size of sand creates air spaces, which allow water to move through the soil, flushing nutrients away from the roots. The soil may become more acidic and dry out as a result, which in turn can limit the availability of the remaining nutrients. This can create a 'hungry' soil, dependent on feeds. The secret is to regularly add organic matter in the form of compost, well-rotted manure and/or green manures (see p.208). Get it right and a well-balanced, yet tweaked sandy soil can be highly productive.

Clay soils When it comes to drainage, clay soils are at the other end of the spectrum to sandy soils. Clay's small particle size limits air spaces, so these soils hold on to moisture, making it harder to work, easy to compact and slower to warm up in the spring. On the upside, these soils usually have excellent reserves of nutrients – your main task is to free them up by getting air and fibre into the mix. And as with sandy soils, incorporating organic matter helps even out the imbalance and move your soil's character towards the loamy ideal. One thing you should avoid at all costs is damaging the soil structure through compaction. Never be tempted to walk, work or use machinery on a clay soil while it is wet.

Soils developed over limestone and rock These are usually alkaline, stony and fairly shallow. These characteristics combine to seriously limit the range of vegetables you can grow, so it's best to create raised beds (see p.193), infilling with bought-in topsoil, and any other organic matter you can lay your hands on.

Soil pH

This gives an indication of the relative acidity or alkalinity of the soil, which governs much of what happens in your veg patch in two ways. Firstly, plants and soil organisms tend to perform at their best within fairly narrow pH limits. As far as your veg patch is concerned, most are happiest somewhere in the middle of the scale (i.e. reasonably neutral conditions), so the nearer you get to this, the broader the range of veg you can grow. Secondly, pH affects the availability of soil nutrients. Most pertinently for the veg patch, acidic soils often have high nutrient levels but for various reasons your plants are unable to get at them.

If you've gone for a professional soil test, the results will tell you all about the pH and may offer advice about any action you may want to take. There is a good DIY alternative though, with most garden centres selling inexpensive pH testing kits. The process is a simple one: put some soil in the tube supplied, add a few drops of test solution, shake it up and leave it to settle. Comparing the colour of the resulting solution with the colour chart supplied indicates the pH of your soil. Chances are you'll have a result somewhere towards neutral, neither strongly acidic nor alkaline, but if not you may wish to take some action.

With acidic soils the usual course of action is to neutralise the acid by applying an alkali, usually lime in one form or another. Agricultural lime (naturally occurring calcium carbonate) is probably the cheapest form of lime for the grower and it can be applied at any time of the year, although best in late winter. You simply cast it over your patch at the rate suggested on the packet. This method may be slow-acting but this makes its effect on soil pH and fertility (as well as plant growth) both steady and long-lasting. Lime is available from most garden centres, countryside suppliers and specialist businesses, but make sure it comes from a sustainable source.

Very alkaline soils are extremely rare, and while it is possible to rectify them with sulphates of one sort or another, you're highly unlikely to find yourself in this position – even if your soil's starting point is alkaline to a degree. The answer to extreme alkalinity is effectively dilution, by incorporating as much organic matter in the form of compost, topsoil and well-rotted manure as you can lay your hands on.

Few of us have the time, money or inclination to aim for the holy grail of the perfect neutralish loam. Nor should we. It is worth remembering that some plants prefer conditions slightly off-centre anyway – potatoes and strawberries like it slightly acid, brassicas slightly alkaline. In practice, as long as you address extremes at the start (or you're planting to suit those conditions) you're likely to find most of what you plant will grow perfectly well. My garden is a little too acidic to be ideal, but although I haven't bothered liming, I do make sure I keep adding organic matter every year. The real point is that with just a slight increase in knowledge about your soil you'll not only understand what's going on in your patch, you'll know what to do about it should you need to. Once you've eliminated any extremes and you're somewhere in the ballpark, my advice is to relax about any limitations, plant appropriately, forget 'perfection', and enjoy the successes and the odd failure.

Creating paths and access

Life will be much easier if you make a very clear distinction between where you grow and where you walk: don't walk on your beds and don't grow your paths. To avoid walking on your beds, make sure they aren't too wide to start with (see p.175), and lay your hands on a couple of wooden planks – old scaffolding boards are ideal, being long and comparatively light. These will allow you to access the middle of your beds but spread the weight of your steps out along its length, minimising compaction. I suggest you chop one of the boards into three sections. You can then use one section if you only want to go a little into the bed, and it means that those less able to manhandle a whole plank can lay out small ones as stepping stones.

The idea of grass paths might sound lovely and green, but unless you have all the time in the world to mow and edge them, forget it. I prefer to dedicate my time to the food. Light-excluding mulch mat makes an immediately effective path; see the directory (pp.265–6) for suppliers. I used mine like that for a couple of months before covering it with a few centimetres of sand and a row of salvaged slabs.

Preparing your beds

Now that your paths are in place, you can set about preparing your beds. Imagine you're a seedling with delicate, fibrous roots branching out in search of anchorage, water and nutrients. The last place you're looking to settle in is a bed full of boulders. You want something soft and fine to nestle into, and if you get it you'll be off to as good a start as you can get.

Once you've cleared your patch of weeds (see p.186), you'll have a choice about how you take your beds to the next stage. You're after a soil of crumble-mix consistency, and there are a few ways of getting there. Hiring a rotovator can be a great timesaver. Churning up the soil as they go, rotovators are the easy way of breaking your soil down to a finer consistency, although they're not without effort on the part of the operator. If you've not used one before, imagine a loud, heavy wheelbarrow with a rather more destructive wheel. Whatever you do though, don't get the rotovator out when the soil is wet, as you'll only smear it and destroy any of the soil structure that you've worked so hard to achieve.

If there's no rotovator option, then I'm afraid there's nothing for it but to bend your back. Any time after the Christmas lights start to go up, dig your patch over to a depth of at least one and a half spits (the height of your spade's blade) and you'll have a few months of rain and frost to weather the lumps down. Around Valentine's Day, when the ground is dry, rake your whole patch over, using the back of the rake or a fork to smash up any remaining clods. Do it well, but not fanatically – it's better to do your whole patch reasonably thoroughly than concentrate madly on a quarter, then lose heart. Rake towards you, taking larger lumps to the side to bash them up some more (or out to the compost bin), then repeat at right angles.

If you have a supply of compost, now's the time to spread it about – this will give it time to start to be taken into the soil by rain and earthworms.

Tagetes and tomatoes in a raised bed

If the idea of so much digging with the upset it causes to the existing soil structure doesn't appeal, or the thought of a little exercise leaves you cold, then you can always opt for the no-dig approach. The method is championed by many who believe that the benefits of digging don't outweigh breaking apart the structure, releasing carbon from the soil and upsetting what may be a healthy ecosystem operating perfectly happily.

One of the most popular no-dig approaches is to lay decomposable material (such as thick cardboard) on the ground and cover it with a layer of compost or topsoil, at least 15cm deep. As well as allowing you to sow or plant directly into the compost layer, the cardboard kills off any weeds and grass before subsequently breaking down. It's a fantastic 'fast-forward' method, and especially effective in colonising areas of lawn. This method, with its mass of added compost or topsoil, creates a raised bed of sorts, but if you're considering the no-dig approach I'd recommend that you create proper raised beds, with sides, as maintenance will be much easier.

Creating raised beds

I love raised beds. An edge around 8–10cm high looks good, makes the cultivated area distinct, and allows you to build up the soil height over time with added compost and organic matter. If it seems like a palaver, let me assure you it's another of those instances where a molehill of work upfront saves a mountain of messing about later on. Not only are edges crisp, it is easy to keep them that way. Strimming and mowing are straightforward, and the edging boards present a pretty decent barrier to weed and grass encroachment.

Raised beds also give you instant good drainage, which is what most plants prefer, and they warm up quickly in the spring allowing you to get on with growing a little earlier. So, if you're on heavy ground or shallow soil or in a cool area, I'd really recommend going for them. That little extra height also helps if you have trouble with (or an inherent resistance to) bending.

Your boards should be at least 13cm wide, 2.5cm thick and the length required. You'll also need some stakes to secure them with: 5 x 5cm and 20cm long should be fine. Allow one stake to screw the boards into in each corner and every metre or so along the sides. As with your walking boards, there are endless sources to choose from (including recycled scaffolding boards), but your nearest sawmill may well prove the best bet for locally sourced wood. Douglas fir is a great one to go for, as it is relatively cheap, looks great and ages beautifully. Also it's one of the harder softwoods, so you can use it without the chemical pressure treatments that are both unsustainable and far from ideal next to where you grow your food.

You can buy your own kits for raised beds, see the directory (p.266) for suppliers. With these, you are up and off almost immediately and you can raise them higher, change bed shapes, pick them up and move them to another site. Not surprisingly, their flexibility makes them popular with many.

Starting off your plants

With your veg patch prepared, you can start the real business of growing some food. You'll be growing most of your vegetables and herbs from seed, every one of which is a little grain of potential. It has all the ingredients within it to become the plant, its flowers and its fruit. Your job is simple: put the seed in contact with a medium that will allow it to reach this potential, when the climate is at its best to suit its needs. Mostly that's a case of sowing it on to some well-prepared ground at a particular time of year, covering it with a thin layer of compost or soil, and watering it.

Occasionally it makes sense to either start plants off indoors or to grow them in protected conditions throughout. In the Vegetable A–Z (pp.20–153), I've outlined what suits each plant best, and where there are options. Of course, you should feel free to try whatever else suits you too.

Getting started outdoors
Sowing the seed straight into your veg patch (direct sowing) is the most time-efficient way of starting off your plants. It misses out the indoor step, any potting on, the increased watering required in the warmer indoors, and saves you time and money.

Direct sowing suits the hardier plants – the salads, spinach, beans and peas, and most of the roots. As long as there is some warmth around, from mid-spring you'll be able to sow these straight into your garden with every chance of success.

Tips for starting your plants outdoors
- Prepare the ground well to give your seeds the best start in life. A fine tilth ensures easy root development
- The smaller the seed, the finer the tilth required. Larger seeds have more reserves and can live with a little hardship on the way if they really have to
- Develop a feeling for where you are. The timings in this book and on the seed packets are a great guide, but there can be a month between the earliest sowings on well-drained soils in the Southwest, and the latest in exposed or heavier soils in the North
- Water the ground lightly before you sow. It stops seed being displaced so easily and speeds germination
- Sow thinly. You can sow large seeds like peas straight from your hand, but smaller seed needs sowing from a pinch – and do it quickly to ensure thinner coverage
- Sow in drills (shallow lines). Even if you are aiming for crops to be in blocks, sow them as a series of rows. It helps ensure good spacing, plus when they start growing, you'll know if it's not in the line it's probably a weed
- Generally the larger the seed, the deeper it is sown. Broad beans to your first knuckle; carrots only with a dusting of covering soil or compost

- The seeds will generally need watering twice a week until they germinate. If the rain doesn't do it for you, fill in the gaps with the watering can
- Thin mercilessly. I have to fight sentimentality every time and remember to think of the ones that are left – they will be healthier, with access to more reserves and space
- Thin the seedlings out to their final spacing when they are a few centimetres tall, and if they are herbs and salad leaves you'll find yourself with a mini-snack to keep you going
- Weed. Weed some more, then weed again. Other plants will compete with your crops for resources, and you don't want them to. So get the hoe out – little and often is best for your sanity. It really is only a chore if you avoid it for a good while. Early in the morning on a sunny day is ideal as the severed weeds will dry up quickly. Give yourself 10 minutes' hoeing every time you go to your patch. You'll be amazed at the immediate transformation, and it will become a pleasant part of your time there
- Every month, make a habit of sharpening your hoe. It will make your weeding so much more pleasurable and efficient

Broad beans emerging

Getting started indoors

It is better to start some plants indoors, or 'under cover' – partly for convenience and in some cases for necessity. Many (such as French beans, tomatoes, courgettes) are not resistant to the cold, so you are unable to sow them outside until the temperature reaches a certain level. Starting them off indoors (in a polytunnel, greenhouse, cloche, or on your windowsill) ensures they have this temperature earlier in the season, and allows you to get them to a reasonable size before you plant them out – when the outdoor temperature is warm enough. And if your plants are ahead, then your harvest will be too.

Also, you may want an earlier crop than from those you sow direct. Peas, beans and salads all get started off in my polytunnel to go outside around the same time as I sow more direct, giving me an earlier crop to go alongside my outdoor-sown one.

Growing under cover gives you much more control over the environment, so you can be more certain that your plants have a gentler start. Strong winds won't be damaging them, and pests aren't given free rein. Germination and survival are usually more successful, so for the extra work before they hit your patch you get extra rewards, and you save the thinning time. They'll also be less vulnerable to the nibblers that like to munch on them. And don't forget, sowing indoors doesn't just provide a protected environment for the plants, it means you are okay to get on with growing when the soil's cold, the weather's wet and the wind's howling.

The chance of your seeds turning into plants and then into delicious food rests very much with their start in life, and the growing medium you choose is a big consideration. Don't mess about, get yourself some good stuff. It needs to be of a fine texture, and of the right nutrient balance, see the directory (pp.265–6) for suppliers. And don't be tempted to go for those growing mediums containing environmentally unsustainable peat. Its extraction releases greenhouses gases and reduces an already endangered and valuable habitat.

Using your compost couldn't be easier. Fill whatever you're sowing into around three-quarters full of compost; this will allow for it to swell when watered. Sow your seed to the depth advised on the packet (see also p.194). It's that simple.

There are a few ways of starting your plants off indoors, each with its own advantages, as follows:

Module trays A great way of starting off your seedlings, these trays are separated into cells, one for each seed. It's simple: the initial spacing is done for you, the plant gets to a good size before it requires moving, and you don't damage any plants when you're taking them out. It's also a great way of starting off all those that hate root disturbance, including most of the brassicas and the Mediterranean favourites like tomatoes. You can always sow two seeds to a cell if you want to be sure of at least one coming up per cell.

Jiffy 7s

Seedlings in a module tray

Jiffy 7s These small cylinders contain a growing medium of coir (recycled coconut fibre) with just about enough nutrients to get your seeds off to a good start. Coming as dehydrated flat counters, a few minutes in water swells them into shape ready to use. Sow one or two seeds into each and keep them watered, preferably in a tray lined with capillary matting to retain moisture. Plant them straight out when the seedlings are 3cm or so high, tearing the tissuey covering a little to let the roots through. Avoid the Jiffy 7s made with peat.

Root trainers Essentially long modules, root trainers are especially suited to plants that enjoy a long root run early in life – the peas and beans in particular. They are worth the investment, or you can take the homemade approach: toilet roll inners filled with compost are cheap and effective, and just as good – with the cardboard decomposing when you plant them out.

Seed trays I am not a great fan of seed trays. With all those plants squashed in together, you damage half of them getting the other half out, and then there's all that separating and potting on. If you really want to use them, remember that when your seedlings have reached 3cm or so tall and have their second pair of leaves, they'll need separating and transferring into a bigger pot, before planting out into your patch when they get to the right size. This is the process known as 'pricking out'. As you try to tease the seedling out of the soil in the seed trays, hold the leaves rather than the stem, as the plants can regrow leaves more easily if they get damaged. You do get more seedlings for less space than in modules so if space is short, seed trays may be for you.

Guttering Sarah Raven introduced me to the idea of using guttering to raise seedlings indoors and I can't recommend it highly enough. It may seem a touch ridiculous at first, but this method really does pay off. All you do is saw the guttering to the length that you want, fill it with compost and sow in the usual way. Try it. Its semi-circular profile saves compost, fits on a windowsill, and is cheap to get hold of. On top of that, guttering *feels* right. It sits in your hands perfectly, making carrying your seedlings about simpler. I also think that the extra surface area of black plastic treats your emerging plants to a little extra heat too. Everything about it makes sense: the compost is concentrated where the plant needs it, watering is reduced as a result, and you can either gently ease the whole length of seedling-filled compost into a prepared ditch in your plot, or tear them off one at a time for planting out.

Pots These use a lot of compost compared to the other methods, so I tend to use them only for the big-seeded cucurbits which appreciate the extra room from the off. For starting your plants off, you have a choice between biodegradable and plastic pots. Coir pots are made from an otherwise unused by-product of the coconut industry and on the face of it are excellent green alternatives to plastic (i.e. oil-based)

Growing seedlings in guttering

containers. However, their green credentials are partly compromised by the distance they travel to reach you and the fact that they are designed to biodegrade. Although this sounds like an advantage, it actually means that all the energy that goes into their creation is used only once. Being 'green' is rarely black and white. Sturdy plastic pots can, of course, be used again and again. I can't make up my mind which is greener, so I tend to use some of each. It's worth remembering that some garden centres will take (and make available) pots for recycling.

Tips for getting off to a good start indoors
• Get your timing right. Refer to the Vegetable A–Z (pp.20–153) for sowing times for each plant. Although the seasons are famously unpredictable, a useful guide is to work back 5 or 6 weeks from when you'd normally expect the last frost and sow then. This gives just the right length of time for the plants to establish themselves before going out into the big wide world with confidence
• As with outside, sow thinly – that way you'll avoid having to thin too much
• Water very, very lightly until your seeds germinate. Try one of those misters usually used for cacti. You want moist but not wet soil, as seeds can easily rot
• For smaller seeds, put your pot (or whatever you're sowing in) on a tray and pour water into the tray – the water soaks up into the pot, which avoids disturbing the delicate seeds
• If you can see roots at the bottom of your chosen container it's time to plant them out. If the weather's not right, then you'll have to pot them on

Planting out
When your seedlings reach the right size, indicated in the Vegetable A–Z (pp.20–153), they are ready to be planted out, and this is the point at which they are at their most vulnerable. As with children heading off to their first day at school, anything you can do to smooth the transition the better it will be for them, and in turn for you.

Any plants started off under cover will benefit from hardening off. For 4 or 5 days take them outside in the day, and get them back under cover for the night. They'll get accustomed to the shift in conditions and be less shocked when planted out.

Water your seedlings well an hour or so prior to planting out, and, if possible, plant them out in the early morning. This will give them all day to get used to their new home, enjoy the sun and get ready for the dark, cooler evening.

Dig the hole or trench *before* you ease the seedling out of its first home, to avoid it drying out – even a little. And do take great care when extracting your seedlings from whatever they've begun life in. If you've sown into modules, gently squeeze around each cell from beneath and (if you have to lend a persuasive tug) grab hold of a leaf (it can grow another) rather than the stem.

Once in place, firm the soil around your seedling, and water in well.

Maintaining your
Veg Patch

Ensuring your veg patch is at its fittest is largely a matter of developing some good habits. You'll need to look after the soil, take care of the plants and keep a regular eye out for pests. Keep this hierarchy in mind and you'll give yourself every chance of a healthy and productive plot.

Your focus should be very much on the soil, as it is the cornerstone of maintaining your veg patch. Organic matter in general and compost in particular are vital to its health. Take the time to learn how to make compost and use other forms of organic matter (see pp.207–10) and you'll encourage a balanced environment for growth. As a consequence, your plants will be healthier, and less troubled by pests. You'll also ensure that, as the years roll by, your soil increases in vitality and health, rather than diminishes.

Once in a while the plants themselves will require your attention – some will need supporting, or an extra feed to help them keep pumping out their harvest. Mostly it's a matter of detail, but it can make all the difference to maximising your harvests, so take time to become familiar with ways of lending your plants a helping hand (see pp.211–15).

Once in a while, despite your best efforts, the pests will come and you will need to know how to deal with them, though you are unlikely to encounter a biblical plague. Pests are more inclined to be quietly tedious – so it's best to be quietly tedious back. Get out there every few evenings and you'll spot them early and be able to deal with them quickly. I've included a guide to recognising and dealing with the main nuisances (see pp.216–19).

If you find yourself looking for the section on pesticides, weedkillers and man-made fertilisers, I'm afraid I'll have to disappoint you. Given that these cause long-term harm for short-term gain, there's no reason to carry on growing that way. In any event it's easy not to, it's healthier not to, and – as endless studies show – yields from organic growing are typically higher over time.

Looking after your soil

The act of growing, for the most part, takes from your soil. As well as using sunlight and water for growth and development, your plants draw in nutrients from the soil (such as nitrogen and potassium) in order to produce the roots, leaves, stems and flowers that you eat. Rotation helps to keep this reduction in soil reserves to a minimum, but the nutrient cycle will spiral downwards unless you step in and play an active part in replenishing it, and that means putting a few sustainable practices in place from the start.

The best ways to do this are to make your own compost and to grow nourishing crops, known as green manures, between your main harvests.

Compost

Nosing through Jane Perrone's excellent *Allotment Keeper's Handbook*, I was slapped across the face by a Bette Midler quote:

'My whole life had been spent waiting for an epiphany, a manifestation of God's presence, the kind of transcendent, magical experience that lets you see your place in the big picture. And that is what I had with my first compost heap.'

I'd been wondering how to convey the enormity of what composting is all about, to try and tie what is on the face of it a faintly ridiculous, grubby little pastime with our place in the world, and our world's place in the whatever, and I have to confess I was struggling. The last thing I was prepared for was Bette Midler doing it in a few dozen well-chosen words.

Compost is about the best all-round treatment you can give your soil. It boosts nutrient status, helps retain moisture, improves soil structure and if laid straight on top of your soil makes a wonderful mulch. Most of what your household throws out can go in it, and that's the beauty of making compost. You're turning the waste from today's meal into something that nurtures your supper tomorrow. Added to that, you're cutting down the contribution to landfill.

Making a compost bin

Strictly speaking you don't need a bin to make your own compost, but in reality it is easier to contain and manage your compost if you do. Plastic bins look neat and are an instant solution – your local council may offer them at a reasonable price. Alternatively, you can also make your own.

The simple, classic design is for a square enclosure with a front that can be opened to make adding material easy. The cheapest construction uses wooden pallets or corrugated iron securely fixed in place to form three of the sides, with a front of wooden slats or another pallet (loosely tied in place) for access. It functions satisfactorily, especially to get you started in producing your own compost. If, however, you're looking for something a little more aesthetically pleasing and with a longer lifespan, then you can create sturdy wooden compost bins without huge expense or any tools other than a saw and a hammer.

Having one compost bin in your garden will work perfectly well, but you need to keep turning the compost in order to aid decomposition. In an ideal world, it is best to have three adjacent bins, as this makes turning easy and ensures that compost that's almost ready to use isn't being added to. The process is simple: use the first bin to add to, then when it's full, turn it into the second bin and begin filling the first with new material. Keep turning the compost in bin 2 from time to time, watering as you do so – this will accelerate the decomposition dramatically. When it's almost ready (or bin 1 becomes full), turn bin 2 into bin 3, and use when it's ready.

Siting your bin on a level, well-drained sunny spot on top of soil allows excess water to get out, worms to get in, and the sun to warm it and speed up the process of decomposition. If concrete is your only option, start the bin off with a layer of soil or (if you have it) your own compost – this will bring in the worms and ensure a population of beneficial organisms gets to work.

Making compost isn't tricky. It's something that will happen anyway – try stopping a potato peeling from decomposing. All you need do is foster the conditions for it to happen quickly and efficiently, and you'll have brown gold aplenty.

Suitable material for your compost bin

Your compost bin will happily convert much of what you'd otherwise throw out into compost, but a little organisation will make it happen quickly and efficiently. Think of your ingredients as belonging to one of two groups: the Greens and the Browns.

The Greens are rich in nitrogen and many are activators that stir the slower-rotting Browns into quicker action. These prime greens include:
• Diluted urine (half a pint of urine to a gallon of water)
• Grass cuttings
• Nettles
• Comfrey leaves

Other Greens you should happily add include:
• Raw vegetable peelings
• Tea bags and coffee grounds
• Young annual weeds, but avoid weeds with seeds at all costs
• Unwoody prunings
• Animal manure from herbivores such as cows and horses (organic is ideal)
• Poultry manure and bedding

The Browns are carbon-rich, and slower to rot than the Greens, but the incorporation of the Green activators breaks them down at a fair pace. The Browns include:
• Waste paper – shredded or torn up is best
• Cardboard
• Bedding from vegetarian pets such as rabbits
• Tough hedge clippings
• Woody prunings – shredded or chopped is best
• Old bedding plants
• Sawdust and wood shavings
• Bracken
• Fallen leaves

'Reuse' comes above 'recycle' in the environmental hierarchy, so where possible it's greener to pass the magazines to your local doctor or dentist for others to read rather than putting them in your compost.

There are a few very definite no-gos when it comes to your compost bin. Meat, fish, dairy and cooked food (including bread) are all likely to attract pests, especially rats. Cat litter and dog faeces can bring any number of parasites and unwanted organisms into your food chain. Avoid putting these in your bin at all costs. Although some plant diseases will be killed off in your compost heap, I tend to lean towards safety and tie any infected plants in a bin bag along with nutrient-rich perennial weeds such as docks, leaving them to break down for a few months (until the larger weeds are unrecognisable) before adding it to the compost heap. Quarantining them in this way means you kill them off no matter how long it takes, rather than leaving a hostage to fortune in your compost.

Any wood shavings, especially if from shredded conifers, not only take a while to decompose in the heap but (if they haven't completely broken down in the compost) can also lock up valuable soil nitrogen, depriving your precious plants for at least a season. It's best to add shavings only in small quantities along with Green activators, or if you have the space, leave them in a pile for a couple of years to break down. Avoid using them at all if the wood has been treated with preservatives. The golden rule in adding to your compost heap is 'if in any doubt, leave it out'.

Wooden compost bins

With compost (as with most things) the more you put in the more you get out. Generally your compost will be ready in 9 months to a year, but if you're after a quick turnaround it can be made in as little as 2 months. The secret is in the turning. The more you mix your compost, or turn it into a neighbouring compost bin, the more air gets incorporated, and air is exactly what decomposing organisms love. Air and water that is. As you turn your compost, give it a good watering, even better if you can make that from your own (ahem) personal tap.

The amalgamated ingredients will begin to break down, reducing in volume, and gradually turning dark brown when the process is complete. It may not be as crumbly and lump-free as you're used to seeing in compost bags from the garden centre, but as long as it is sweet-smelling and earthy it will be perfectly usable. If you can sieve it or pull out any big bits (such as twigs) then do, and return them to your bin to break down some more.

Tips for the best compost

Given time, even the most clumsily constructed pile will decompose, but if you're after the finest compost there is, here are a few steps to help you along the way:

• Use more or less equal volumes of Greens and Browns, but your own mix will need to take into account your site, the weather and the time you're able to put into it – learn from your experiences, and remember...

• Greens and Browns regulate each other: if your compost is too wet, add more Browns; if it's too dry, add some Greens

• Ensure that you don't use too thick a layer of either at once – the best compost is formed most efficiently when Greens and Browns are as integrated as possible

• Use green activators like grass cuttings to activate otherwise slow-rotting Browns

• Don't shy away from using some of the tougher Browns. They may break down more slowly on their own, but in combination with the Greens they provide essential bulk and structure to your finished product. If you maximise their surface area by chopping or shredding, you'll find the accelerating Greens will nudge them along

• If you can, have three bins side by side and keep turning and watering them.

Speeding up your compost

If you're feeling particularly enthused and want to make fantastic compost in record time, you can always have a bash at adding a bit of heat to your heap. The principles are the same as for any compost, but the smaller you shred your material before adding it to the heap the better, as this creates a greater surface area for decomposition to take place. Shears are good for chopping up small amounts, but for woodier material, if your mower is sturdy enough, make a low pile and mow over it to take it down a grade or two. If you've a lot to get through, consider hiring a chipper.

The key to heat is thorough and frequent mixing, and ensuring everything is damp as you do it, as the two big agents of decomposition are water and air. After a week or so you'll notice the heap is getting warm. This is a good sign, as it indicates biological action is under way. It may even get positively hot – a neighbour even baked a potato in his (it took only a couple of hours to cook through).

A week or two later the compost may start to cool. As soon as you notice this turn it again, trying to get the centre of the heap to the outside and vice versa. Add more water (or urine) if you need to, or more material if it is more than damp. The heap should warm up well again as the aerobic organisms get back to full steam. You can repeat this a few times if you want, but at some stage the heating effect will diminish. When you reach this stage, you can leave the heap to finish off by itself.

You can add compost at any time of the year, but a month or two before spring kicks in will ensure your beds get a much-needed boost for the hard work ahead.

Other sources of organic matter

The ideal is to create a closed system of nutrients for your veg patch, whereby your life adds all the nutrients to rebalance those taken out by the plants you eat, but sometimes practical considerations make it unattainable. Luckily, there are endless off-site sources for organic matter that will enrich your soil.

Farmyard manure Full of beneficial nutrients, source it from an organic holding if you can. You'll need to let it compost well (for at least 6 months) before you add it to your patch, to allow it to settle chemically and biologically. This also allows time for any worming treatments to degrade – they don't just kill the animals' worms, they'll do for earthworms too!

Chicken manure Very high in nutrients, this is best added to your compost to dilute it, rather than added direct to your soil, as it can be very concentrated.

Mushroom compost Having been used for growing mushrooms, this spent compost is low in nutrients but an excellent source of fibre for the soil, helping its structure and in so doing raising the availability of the nutrients in it. It may be mildly alkaline, so not the one to go for if you're on chalky ground (see p.189).

Seaweed Pick a carrier bag full of this potassium-rich plant yourself if you live near the coast, washing it clean of salt, before adding it to the surface as an excellent feeding mulch. Or you can mix into your compost bin.

Straw, hay, grass and old animal bedding From chickens and pigs, these are good sources of organic matter, but best added to your compost to decompose first.

Green manures

This magical group of plants acts as a living manure, soil improver and/or fertiliser. They tend to be short-term crops that grow a mass of foliage rapidly, covering the soil and suppressing weeds, thereby minimising erosion, nutrient leaching and compaction. On top of that, some green manures root deeply, aerating the soil, drawing minerals to the surface and helping to break up the ground, which is particularly useful if you have clay soil. Some (such as clover) belong to the legume family, taking nitrogen from the air and making it available in the soil to feed the vegetables that follow. When you need the space again, your green manures can then be composted or dug in to improve soil structure.

There are many green manures to choose from to suit your purpose, although they are particularly good to grow over winter, acting like a duvet for the soil as well as improving its structure and fertility through what for many are the least productive months. The table opposite covers the best green manures, an idea of when to use them and the benefits they offer.

Crimson clover

Green manure	Sow	Cut/Dig in	Nitrogen fixer?	Characteristics
Agricultural lupins	March–June	Sept–Nov	Yes	Does well in an acid soil. Treat as a legume in the rotation.
Agricultural mustard	March–Sept	Sept–Nov	Yes	Very fast-growing, giving good quick coverage. Treat as a brassica in the rotation.
Alfalfa	May–July	3 months later or overwinter	Yes	Rich in elements needed for good growth. Treat as a legume in the rotation.
Buckwheat	April–Aug	3 months later or longer	No	Very quick-growing. Flowers attract beneficial insects. Does well on poor ground (which it improves).
Crimson clover	March–Aug	3 months later or overwinter	Yes	Flowers attract beneficial insects (especially bees). Treat as a legume in the rotation.
Field beans	Sept–Nov	After winter	Yes	Excellent coverage.
Hungarian grazing rye	Aug–Sept	March–May	No	Good, quick coverage.
Phacelia	March–Sept	3 months later or overwinter in the South	No	Beautiful flowers that attract beneficial insects, especially bees. Quick, tall growth.
Red clover	April–Aug	2 months to 2 years later	Yes	Flowers attract beneficial insects. Ideal for growing long term. Treat as a legume in the rotation.
Tares	March–Sept	March–May	Yes	Excellent fertility builder. Treat as a legume in the rotation.
White clover	April–Aug	3 months later or longer	Yes	Low-growing. Flowers attract beneficial insects. Ideal for growing long term. Treat as a legume in the rotation.

Mulches

A mulch is simply any layer of material placed on the surface of the soil. Its primary role is to suppress weeds, but most mulches help to retain water in summer, reduce run off in winter, deter pests, and limit temperature fluctuations simply by acting as an insulating blanket. There are endless possibilities to choose from. Flattened cardboard boxes do the basic job perfectly well, but compost is the best all-rounder – bringing all of those benefits while adding nutrients and improving soil structure as it gradually works its way into the soil (or rather rain and worms work it in for you). Hay, straw, seaweed and spent mushroom compost are also excellent choices, working well as suppressors, barriers and insulators but they usually need clearing away, composting and replacing after a while.

Loose mulches are easy to use. Water the ground well first to ensure the soil has a good initial reserve, then spread a reasonable layer (at least 5cm) of your mulch around your plants to reap the benefits. If you have large uncultivated areas or are leaving a bed (or even your whole plot) without crops for a while, then you're best going for a living mulch in the form of a green manure (see p.208). Anywhere that requires long-term mulching, such as paths, will need a more durable covering. Permeable, breathable, hardwearing mulch mat is ideal, and comes in rolls of anything from 1–5-metre widths, see the directory (pp.265–6) for suppliers.

Squash growing through biodegradable cornstarch mulch

Looking after your plants

The best thing you can do to promote healthy plants is to look after the soil. The rest is largely detail, but in the detail lies the few per cent that can make all the difference. Some plants require physical support while they attempt to scramble skywards for the space, light and ventilation they need to deliver a really bountiful crop.

It also helps to understand companion planting (see p.212), whereby plants work in sweet partnership, often to mutual advantage. Learning to foster these happy alliances will do much to maximise your harvest and minimise the pests.

There are also a few highly productive food factories, like courgettes and beans, which really benefit from a nutritious boost to keep them at maximum productivity. You don't need to rush out and buy these, all you need is a few nettles (easy to source) or a corner dedicated to the marvel that is the comfrey plant.

Supporting plants

Although most of your plants will happily throw out edible bits for you to feast on, the odd one will need a little help on its way to harvest time. Most peas, some beans, and a few varieties of sweetcorn will all be grateful of either canes, netting or twine to help them keep to the vertical. Where possible, take advantage of what's already there. Grow climbers along a wire fence, tack a little netting to a wall or try the Three Sisters method (see p.180).

If you're growing rows of climbers, push canes or stakes of at least 2-metre length into the ground a few centimetres away from your seedling or the place you intend to plant it, tying them together at the top with their opposite cane. What you'll end up with is a triangular tunnel with your plants growing up the sides.

Another way that looks beautiful and is equally suitable for pot growing is training your climbers up a tepee. Spacing will vary a little depending on your crop, but 30cm between stakes is usual, with two plants growing up each cane. Push the stakes in well, and tie them together at the top – preferably leaving one 'side' open to form a C shape, so that you can get to the inside to harvest any crops before they over-mature. If you have it to hand, hazel lengths work really well, otherwise bamboo canes are probably your cheapest option. A tip I picked up from Simon Hansford, head gardener before me at River Cottage, is to grow beans on an 'X' frame so that the beans hang on the outside of the canes, making harvesting easier. Whatever you're growing, using whatever supporting system, plant on the inside of the canes as you're less likely to damage the plants with the hoe or your size 10s.

Dwarf varieties supposedly do perfectly well without support, but many (especially peas) will benefit from some of the twiggier hazel growth pushed fat end into the soil, lending the tendrils something to latch on to and preventing any pods trailing along the ground.

Companion planting

This technique of growing plants in close proximity with the aim of benefiting at least one of them is enchanting. Careful partnering can achieve so many ends. Sow in the right combinations and you'll attract beneficial insects to your patch for pollinating flowers and hoovering up aphids; you'll be able to disguise the scent of crops vulnerable to pests that navigate by smell, accumulate otherwise unavailable minerals and/or nitrogen for neighbouring or subsequent crops, or simply provide physical help such as shelter and support. Some (such as nasturtiums) even lay down their leaves, to attract pests away from the crop destined for your kitchen.

For the organic vegetable grower, companion planting ranks alongside rotation and soil health as one of your foremost weapons against pests and diseases, so it pays to know a little about it. I've noted some of the more commonly used companions earlier, but the table opposite should help influence your planting plans. It won't leave you pest-free, but it will form a harmonious, eco-friendly first line of defence. And once you start exploring the possibilities of companion planting, you'll be hooked.

If you only have time to experiment with a few companions in your first year then try the following:

- Plant spring onions or chives in with your carrots – carrot fly can smell carrots from up to a mile away, but the onion family mask their carroty smell
- Plant basil near your tomatoes as it attracts aphids to it, and away from your precious tomatoes
- Sow nasturtiums near your beans and lettuces – they are a great sacrificial plant, attracting cabbage white butterflies away from your more precious harvests.

Pot marigold attracting pollinators to the veg patch

Companion	Companion for	Benefit
Onion family	Many vegetables	Disguises the scents of other vulnerable harvests, notably protecting carrots from carrot fly
Basil	Tomatoes, aubergines	Attracts aphids away from more vulnerable harvests
Borage	Tomatoes, squash	Attracts pollinating insects and repels tomato worm
Coriander	Most vegetables	Repels aphids and carrot fly, and attracts bees when allowed to flower
Hyssop	Brassicas	Repels cabbage white butterflies and attracts pollinating insects if allowed to flower
Marigolds (*Tagetes* sp.)	Most vegetables	Produces chemicals in its roots, which deter nematodes, slugs and wireworms
Mint	Cabbage, tomatoes, radish	Deters cabbage white butterflies, aphids and flea beetles
Nasturtiums	Brassicas	Attract cabbage white butterflies away from brassicas and lettuces
Nettles	Legumes and brassicas	Attract aphids and cabbage white butterflies away from legumes and brassicas
Oregano	Brassicas	Repels cabbage white butterflies, and attracts beneficial insects when flowering
Pot marigold (*Calendula officinalis*)	Tomatoes, asparagus	Repels tomato worm, whitefly and asparagus beetle
Rosemary	Legumes, brassicas, carrots	Repels cabbage white butterflies, bean beetle and carrot fly, and attracts beneficial insects when flowering
Sage	Brassicas, carrots, radish	Repels cabbage moth, carrot fly, and flea beetle
Thyme	Brassicas	Attracts beneficial insects when flowering, and may repel whitefly, cabbage worms

Comfrey

Comfrey feeds

Looking a little like untidy borage, comfrey grows rapidly with roots that drive deep down into the soil, dragging otherwise inaccessible minerals up to accumulate above ground. It is these reserves that make comfrey such a star in your garden. Nitrogen, potassium and phosphorus form the holy trinity of nutrients that most plant growth depends on, and comfrey has them in abundance.

Forget the artificial chemicals. Growing comfrey is a natural, cut-and-come-again way of adding a few nutrients while you water. Its quick-growing nature makes for a natural fertiliser factory, which you can utilise in a number of ways. Cut leaves, laid as a mulch, will gradually liberate their minerals as they break down, or act as a wonderful accelerator if incorporated into your compost heap, but I use comfrey most as a liquid feed.

Making your own comfrey feed is simple: fill an old onion net or similar with torn-up comfrey leaves and suspend it in your water butt. Over the next few weeks it will decompose in the water to create comfrey tea. I'll warn you, it smells like a tram driver's glove, but you'll soon learn to love it when you see the lift it gives to any of your fruiting plants – tomatoes, courgettes and beans in particular will thank you for a drink of it. Give them a good watering, or spray the leaves, any time from flowering onwards and they will repay you with a heftier harvest.

If you do not have a water butt, chop the bottom off a large upturned water bottle and fill it with comfrey leaves, placing half a brick or something similar on top to keep the leaves under pressure. Over the next week or two, they will begin to breakdown and leach their dark liquid into the neck. Then you simply undo the lid, decant, and dilute the goo with water in the ratio of 15:1 for use. You can also make tea in the same way using nettles, though their chemical balance is more towards nitrogen (good for growth) than potassium (best for fruiting), so use it when it's growth that you want to encourage. Bought seaweed feeds do a similar job but they are comparatively costly.

There are a number of varieties of comfrey, but lay your hands on the Bocking 14 comfrey if you can, see the directory (pp.265–6) for suppliers. It's a sterile variety and therefore doesn't set seed, which allows you to control its footprint (comfrey can be very invasive). If you want to expand your supply of this marvellous resource, dig up a root in winter and slice it into counters the thickness of a pound coin. Sow each counter 3cm deep in a pot filled with compost. Roots will soon form, ready for planting out any time from late spring.

It's hard not to be a little evangelical about comfrey once you start using it and see the results. It has the big-hitting macronutrients that are essential for plant growth, it looks amazing and its flowers bring endless beneficial insects to your plot. And it's pretty much free.

Pests and diseases

Pests and diseases could fill a whole (admittedly rather dull) book of their own. That said, the main threats to the frequency and enormity of your haul are largely predictable, easy to identify and few in number. If you rotate your crops and look after the soil, and pair up your crops with their helpful companions you will be giving yourself every chance of minimising troubles, but some pest and disease tedium comes with the territory.

I've tried to cover the most probable causes, along with prevention and any remedies, for each of the foods in the Vegetable A–Z (pp.20–153), and gone into further detail below about the most likely troublemakers. But there will come a time when something cleans you out of a tasty crop – the one you were most looking forward to, no doubt. It's rare, but it happens. Learn what you can from it, but get used to it: pests and diseases are part of life's rich travesty in the veg patch.

If you're unfortunate enough to turn up some weird malady that doesn't seem to fit these descriptions, don't be shy of getting on the internet if you have access. Any number of sources will be able to help you, see the directory (see pp.265–6) for a few starting points. Otherwise this is where having signed up to a club or society, or growing on a shared space, really comes into its own. Bending the ear of fellow allotmenters or gardeners is all part of the sociable fun of it.

Slugs and snails These will almost certainly be your number one enemy, clearing vast tracks of seedlings and stripping larger leaves to their bones. In my experience there is no universal panacea when it comes to dealing with them – so hit them with a range of methods for limiting their number. Copper tape gives them an electric shock (it cheers my heart just to read those words), but is usually impractical for defending your whole patch. Still, if you've any particularly precious plants in smaller beds or pots this is well worth investing in. Slug pubs are another favourite: sink a yoghurt carton or similar down to soil level and fill it with beer, which seems to attract the slimemakers for one last drink in the saloon before they fall in and drown. It's what 3 per cent lager was made for.

There are biological controls available to you as well, see the directory (p.266) for suppliers. Most are tiny nematodes, worms that are harmless to us and delightfully harmful to slugs in particular. They can be expensive if you're relying on them to police a large area, but excellent for particularly intensive or smaller areas. Slugs and snails are not overly keen on sandy, gritty surfaces, although I usually find that the simple act of gardening soon covers the grit I've put down. If you ask me there's little to beat dusk patrol, harvesting them in a bucket for the chickens or snipping them in half. You need to get used to them too, they'll always be there – but if you hit them hard and keep knocking them back (and accept a little loss here and there) the balance of things will remain on your side.

Common striped snail

Cabbage white caterpillar

Caterpillars Butterflies, especially the cabbage white, come to your plot looking for somewhere to lay their eggs; more specifically they're looking for a food supply for the caterpillars that will eventually emerge. Luckily for you, it's pretty much just one corner of your patch that flashes 'Caterpillar food' to them in huge neon lights – the brassicas. If you've too much time on your hands then here's an excuse to buy one of those pocket-sized identification books, otherwise you'll be happy to know that caterpillar ID is irrelevant to the remedy – here we have the perfect daytime use for your dusk patrol slug bucket. Birds will help you out to some degree, but there's no substitute for regular checks. And don't wait for the caterpillars, go looking for the eggs as soon as you see the butterflies about and rub them off. Fine netting can work in excluding butterflies, but I hate that barrier between me and the plants so I don't bother with it.

Aphids Most aphids will come to your plot in the form of tiny green- and blackfly. You'll find they mainly target soft young growth in spring, the underside of new leaves and growth tips in particular. For the most part they are a relatively harmless nuisance, but if they establish in larger numbers they can seriously weaken a plant, as well as passing on diseases as they move from plant to plant. You're much less likely to encounter them in numbers if you encourage their natural predators to set up house on your plot. It's the lacewings, ladybirds, hoverflies and the like that you're after, so get the flowers and the companion plants in that attract them. You may also want to consider investing in horticultural fleece to cover the most vulnerable plants and exclude the aphids in the process.

If aphids still show up – and sometimes they will – just rub or hose them off, or if they are really persistent, use horticultural soft soap made from naturally occurring fatty acids.

Asparagus beetle and flea beetle

Both may nibble at your crops, but rarely do serious damage. That said, nothing should mess with asparagus. Pick off and destroy any asparagus beetles, and burn end-of-season foliage to prevent them overwintering. Try Bob Flowerdew's inspired method for dealing with flea beetle: smear a square of cardboard with treacle and wave it just above the leaves. This causes the disturbed beetle to leap up and stick to the card, for you to take off and feed to the chickens or throw on the fire – brilliant.

Asparagus beetle

Soil worms Wireworms and cutworms can be a nuisance, although luckily they rarely reach more troublesome status. Wireworms are the larvae of a group of click beetles that like to channel into roots, potatoes in particular. This can lead to rotting, or at least act as a guide hole for slugs to excavate. Cutworms are the larvae of specific moths and they do as you'd expect from their name, slicing off the roots of vulnerable seedlings. Both are easy to detect from their damage, and tend to be more of a problem in plots that were previously grass.

A little damage is almost inevitable although early lifting of crops, such as potatoes, helps limit wireworm damage. But, if you feel that the balance has swung a touch too much away from you, then try digging your patch over when it's convenient to expose the pests to hungry birds. If wireworms really get out of hand (this is reassuringly rare) there's always the nematode (*Heterorhabditis megadis*) route for you to try. August or September is the best time to use it as the wireworms are hatching, and bear in mind that you may have to repeat its use the following year.

If you detect cutworm damage, then carefully dig around the affected plant. You'll usually discover cutworms near the soil surface – destroy them as you find them. They feed (and do their damage) at night, so keep on the lookout for them above ground at dusk.

Blight If your potatoes, tomatoes or any of the other Solanaceae family develop brown blotches on their leaves, get ready to act – your plants have been infected by the fungal disease *Phytophthora infestans*, or blight. If not caught early, the disease will move on to the rest of the plant, attacking the edible parts you prize most.

Blight needs warmth and moist conditions to spread and is most common in late summer. Spores are spread by wind and rain so indoor crops are rarely affected, but if you're growing Solanaceae outside, then consider sourcing more resistant varieties, such as 'Verity', 'Lady Balfour', 'Cara' and 'Remarka' maincrop potatoes; 'Legend' and 'Ferline' (F1) tomatoes, and/or early-maturing varieties, which are likely to be harvested before blight is a threat.

If blight strikes, chop back and burn the foliage in the hope that it hasn't spread to the roots. Allow 3 weeks for the spores on the surface to die (and the skins of your tubers to thicken a little more) before digging them up.

Hygiene is vital. Ensure good air circulation indoors, get your seed from a reputable supplier and, to be on the safe side, don't save any seed for the following year. With potatoes, it is important to remove every single scrap of plant and root you can find, even when harvesting an unaffected crop as the merest morsels can potentially harbour blight. They may regrow into rogue potato plants, known as 'volunteers', that can infect your subsequent crop. If you spot any volunteers that have sprung up from remnants of last year's harvest, dig them up and burn them. It pays to be meticulous.

Recipes

Half the garden soup

What better way to start off the recipes than this wonderfully adaptable celebration of high harvest on your veg patch? You won't need to use any stock as the vegetables add so much flavour of their own. Apart from the tomatoes and onions, all the headliners can be substituted for whatever you have plenty of. From late August onwards, you can add whatever fresh beans are about. Apart from the lovely borlotti, try a few beans plucked from overgrown French or runner bean pods – just give any beans a few minutes' cooking time before you add the other vegetables.

Serves 4–6

A little olive oil or butter
500g onions, peeled and sliced
½–1kg ripe tomatoes
Sea salt and freshly ground
  black pepper

Some or all of the following
3–4 medium carrots, peeled and diced
3–4 medium beetroot, peeled and
  diced
3–4 medium courgettes, diced

A few handfuls of peas
A fistful of French or runner beans,
  roughly chopped
A fistful of chard or spinach leaves,
  finely shredded
A fistful of kale or cabbage leaves,
  finely shredded

To serve
Extra virgin olive oil, to drizzle

Heat a little olive oil or butter in a large pan and sweat the onions until softened. Meanwhile put the tomatoes into a bowl, pour on boiling water to cover and leave for a minute, then drain and peel off the skins. Chop roughly and add to the onions. Cook gently for about 15 minutes until thick and pulpy, then add about 500ml cold water (or light stock) and a good pinch of salt.

Now add the vegetables of your choice, except the leafy veg. Bring to the boil, lower the heat and simmer for 10 minutes. Now add the shredded leafy veg and top up with a little more boiling water if necessary. Simmer for another 5 minutes, stirring regularly, until all the vegetables are tender, but only just.

Taste and adjust the seasoning, then serve immediately, in warm bowls. Drizzle a little olive oil over each serving.

Variations

Pretty much any harvest you have available can be swapped for a similar weight of one of the same family: 3–4 medium parsnips instead of 3–4 carrots, for example.

Curried root soup

It may be a bit strange to start by telling you to ignore the recipe, but that's what I'm going to do here. Well, not ignore it exactly, but do adjust the veg to suit yourself and what you have to hand. Just make sure that you end up with about 700g roots and potato, chopped into 2cm (or so) cubes. No parsnips? Substitute 200g turnips, or up the other vegetables slightly, and so on. This is just a great basic recipe for creating a tasty, satisfying soup and I do hope you'll make it your own.

Serves 4

1 tbsp olive oil
1 large onion, peeled and
    finely chopped
4 garlic cloves, peeled and sliced
1 thumb-sized piece of fresh root
    ginger, peeled and chopped
1 tsp cumin seeds, ground
1 tsp caraway seeds, ground
1 tsp coriander seeds, ground
3 tsp medium curry powder
200g carrots, peeled and chopped
200g celeriac, peeled and chopped

200g parsnip, peeled and cut
    into small dice
100g potato, peeled and chopped
1.5 litres light vegetable stock (see
    p.259) or chicken stock
Sea salt and freshly ground pepper

To serve
1 tbsp chopped coriander leaves
Natural yoghurt, flavoured with a
    little chopped mint
Flat breads or naan

Heat the olive oil in a large saucepan over a medium heat. Add the onion, garlic, ginger, ground spices and curry powder. Fry gently, stirring frequently, for 5–10 minutes until the onions are soft, then add the chopped roots and potato. Cook gently for another 10 minutes.

Add the stock and bring to a simmer, then cover the pan and simmer gently until all the vegetables are tender, about 15 minutes.

Purée the soup in a blender, in batches if necessary, until smooth, then return to the pan and heat through. Taste and adjust the seasoning.

Ladle the soup into warmed bowls, scatter over the chopped coriander and add a little minted natural yoghurt. Serve with some warm flat breads or naan.

Variations
Vary the roots according to what you have available. Just keep the total weight approximately the same, and don't substitute the potatoes.

Lettuce soup with spring onions, broad beans and chorizo

Sweet broad beans and salty, spicy chorizo are made for each other. Easy to prepare, this soup is lovely as a solo treat, yet alluring enough to grace the smartest of dinners. It is delicious served hot or cold.

Serves 4

20g unsalted butter

1 large bunch of spring onions, finely sliced

400ml light vegetable stock (see p.259)

3 lettuces (Cos, Romaine or similar), shredded

250g freshly picked, shelled broad beans

Sea salt and freshly ground black pepper

1 tbsp olive oil

About 60g chorizo sausage, cut into small chunks

To serve

Handful of mint leaves (optional)

Melt the butter in a medium heavy-based saucepan over a low heat. Add the spring onions and cook until soft, about 5 minutes. Pour in the stock and bring to a gentle simmer. Throw in the shredded lettuces and half the broad beans. Allow the lettuce to wilt, giving an occasional stir, then cook for a further 5 minutes.

Purée the soup in a blender, in batches if necessary, until smooth. If it seems a little thick, thin with a dash more stock. Season well with salt and pepper.

Blanch the remaining broad beans in a small pan of boiling water for 2 minutes. If using baby beans, you don't need to skin them; if they're larger, cool slightly, then squeeze them between your finger and thumb until they pop out of their skins.

Heat a frying pan, add the olive oil, then throw in the chorizo and fry until it crisps up. Add the blanched beans and toss to coat in the sausage-seasoned oil.

To serve the soup hot, heat it through and ladle into warm bowls, then top with the fried chorizo and broad beans. Alternatively, cool then chill, adjusting the seasoning before serving, scattered with the broad beans, chorizo and torn mint leaves.

Variations

Although not quite as perfectly as broad beans, peas work very well in this recipe – just throw them in a minute or two before the end.

Jerusalem artichoke soup

Peeling Jerusalem artichokes is a labour of love, owing to their knobbly surfaces, but the intensely earthy and luscious flavour of this soup makes it all worthwhile, I promise. Once peeled, drop them into a bowl of water with a squeeze of lemon juice added, so they don't discolour while you prepare everything else.

Serves 4–6

50g unsalted butter
1kg Jerusalem artichokes, peeled and
   larger ones halved
350g leeks, washed and finely sliced
100g potato, peeled and diced
1 medium onion, peeled and diced
2 garlic cloves, peeled and chopped
750ml good chicken stock or
   vegetable stock (see p.259)

100ml double cream
Sea salt and freshly ground black
   pepper

To serve
Snippets of crisp-fried bacon,
   or 4–6 spoonfuls of pesto
   (see p.258)

Melt the butter in a large, heavy-based saucepan and sweat all the vegetables and the garlic until soft, about 10 minutes. Pour in the stock, bring to the boil, then turn down the heat and simmer for 20–30 minutes until the vegetables are very soft.

Purée the soup in a blender, in batches if necessary, until smooth. Return the soup to the pan and bring to a simmer, then turn down the heat. Stir in the cream and season well with salt and pepper. Warm through, being careful not to let it boil.

Ladle the soup into warm bowls. Scatter over some snippets of crispy bacon or stir a spoonful of pesto into each serving.

Variations

For this creamy soup, you can easily substitute similar veg for the leeks, artichokes and potato, but I'd recommend halving the overall weight of veg if you're not using Jerusalem artichokes. A particularly delicious combination is 500g diced celeriac and 100g each of potato and leeks. If any variation seems slightly too thick once puréed, simply thin with a little milk.

Leek and celeriac soup

I find it incredibly satisfying that a vegetable as unglamorous as celeriac can create a soup which is so elegant and rich. Of course, the addition of oysters makes it particularly sophisticated, but it's also good simply splashed with a little cream and sprinkled with some finely chopped chives.

Serves 6–8

50g unsalted butter
1 tbsp olive oil
About 500g peeled celeriac, roughly chopped (peeled weight)
2 tender inner sticks of celery, chopped
2 leeks, washed and sliced
1 potato (about 150g), peeled and roughly chopped
1 medium onion, peeled and chopped
2 garlic cloves, peeled and chopped

About 1.25 litres light chicken or fish stock, or vegetable stock (see p.259)
½ glass white wine
16 fresh oysters in their shells scrubbed clean (optional)
100ml double cream, plus a little extra
Sea salt and freshly ground black pepper

To serve
Finely chopped chives (optional)

Place a large saucepan over a medium-low heat and add the butter and olive oil. When the butter is foaming, stir in all the chopped vegetables and garlic. Cook gently for about 10 minutes until everything is softened but not coloured. Pour in the stock and wine and bring to a gentle simmer. Cover and cook for 20–25 minutes, stirring once or twice, until all the vegetables are tender.

Purée the soup in a blender, in batches if necessary, until smooth. If it seems a little thick, thin with a bit more stock or water. Return to the pan.

If using oysters, place a large saucepan containing half a glass of water over a high heat and bring to the boil. Place half the oysters in the pan, cover with a tight-fitting lid and allow them to steam for 2 minutes; this will lightly poach the oysters and open the shells just a crack. Remove from the pan and finish the job – carefully opening up the shells and taking the meat out, without spilling the juice in the shell – tip this into a small bowl. Repeat with the remaining oysters.

To finish the soup, stir in the cream and the reserved oyster juice, if including. Warm the soup through gently and season with salt and pepper to taste. Ladle into warm bowls and pop the poached oysters on top or add a splash of cream and a sprinkling of chives to serve.

Minted artichoke houmous

Try to time the making of this dip to coincide with listening to something on the radio, or a new CD. Removing the flesh from the artichokes takes a while, but it's a soothing way of passing the time, and the results are definitely worth it. It might be an unorthodox houmous, but the earthy taste of the artichokes contrasts beautifully with their surprisingly silky, creamy and rich texture. It makes a great dip for veggies and is really delicious spread on bruschetta (see overleaf).

Serves 4–8 as a starter
7–8 globe artichokes
Sea salt and freshly ground black
    pepper
1 garlic clove, peeled and finely
    chopped

Handful of mint leaves,
    roughly chopped
2–3 tbsp olive oil

Add the artichokes to a pan of boiling salted water and cook for 25–40 minutes, depending on size; they are ready when you can pull one of the leaves off easily, and when a knife inserted into the base meets with little resistance.

Leave the artichokes until cool enough to handle, then pick off the leaves. If these have any substantial flesh on them, use a small paring knife or teaspoon to scrape it off and reserve it for the houmous. Once you reach the artichoke's heart, pull off the choke (the hairy immature flower which sits beneath the leaves) and remove any tough or fibrous parts of the stems.

Put the artichoke hearts into a food processor or blender, along with any flesh you have taken from the leaves. Add the garlic and mint. Now pulse, adding enough olive oil through the funnel as you go to give you a thickish consistency – just like that of a traditional chickpea houmous. Season with salt and pepper to taste and serve immediately.

Variations
This is also wonderful with asparagus, broad beans, peas or beetroot replacing the artichoke hearts.

Tomato bruschetta
with blue cheese and confit chilli

Sweet, salty, sharp and punchy – this recipe has it all. You'll need very ripe tomatoes, preferably on the large size: 'Brandywine', 'Black Krim' and 'San Marzano' are ideal. For the cheese, Stilton is good, although Dorset Blue Vinny is worth seeking out.

The intensely flavoured confit chilli oil is particularly special and you'll be glad that the quantities here make more than you need for this recipe. Keep the rest in a sealed bottle in the fridge and use to add zing to salad dressings and marinades.

Serves 4 as a starter or snack

4 slices of good, rustic white bread	For the confit chilli oil
1 garlic clove, peeled	6 mildish chillies, such as
4 ripe tomatoes, sliced	'Poblano'
200g blue cheese	250ml olive oil
Freshly ground black pepper	1 tsp thyme leaves
	1 garlic clove (unpeeled)

To make the confit chilli oil, slice the chillies open from tip to tail, then remove the seeds with a spoon and discard. Slice the chilli into strips and place them in a small saucepan with the olive oil, a few thyme leaves and the unpeeled garlic clove. Heat slowly until the oil is simmering very gently and cook the chillies until soft, about 25 minutes. Remove from the heat and allow the oil to cool.

For the bruschetta, preheat the grill to high. Drizzle or brush a little of the confit chilli oil over the bread slices. Toast on both sides until golden, then rub them all over with the garlic clove.

Place the tomato slices on to the bruschetta, crumble over plenty of blue cheese and flash them under the grill until bubbling. Place on warm plates and season with pepper (the cheese will probably provide enough saltiness). Spoon over a little more of the confit chilli oil and serve immediately.

Variations

All manner of vegetables lend themselves to tasty bruschetta, including roasted peppers, broad bean or borlotti bean purée, and globe artichokes in the form of minted artichoke houmous (see p.229).

Vegetable tempura

The key to creating perfect, crispy tempura is to ensure that the water is very cold and the fat is very hot. Mix the batter just before you want to use it and don't over-mix – a few lumps are fine. In fact, a few lumps are very good as they create extra crunch. Get everything ready to go and whisk up the batter as the oil is heating up.

Serves 4 as a starter or snack

About 1 litre groundnut or vegetable
  oil for deep-frying

For the tempura batter
125g plain flour
Good pinch of sea salt, plus extra
  for sprinkling
1 egg yolk
175ml ice-cold sparkling water

For the vegetables
A selection (or one) of the following:
Sugar snap peas
Baby carrots
Baby beetroot
Cauliflower florets
Broccoli florets
Or anything else you can batter...

Heat a 10cm depth of oil in a suitable deep, heavy-based saucepan until it registers 180°C on a frying thermometer, or until a cube of white bread dropped into the oil turns golden brown in just under a minute.

For the batter, sift the flour and salt together into a large mixing bowl, then whisk in the egg yolk and sparkling water.

Cook the tempura a few pieces at a time: dip the vegetables into the batter to coat and then carefully drop them into the hot oil. Fry for a minute or so until golden brown, using a fork or spoon to drizzle a little more batter over the vegetables as they are frying. Don't overcrowd the pan.

Drain the tempura on kitchen paper, sprinkle with sea salt and serve immediately, while piping hot.

Variations

Try any veg you have to hand. Baby carrots and other tender small roots, and non-leafy harvests are suitable.

Deep-fried courgette flowers

These are surprisingly easy to make once you've mastered the technique, and they look incredibly pretty on the plate. You might also like to try stuffing the courgette flowers with some soft goat's cheese flavoured with a little chopped thyme before coating them in batter and deep-frying, as below.

Serves 3–4 as a starter or snack

12 courgettes, with flowers
A little olive oil
3 garlic cloves, peeled and crushed
Flaky sea salt
About 1 litre sunflower or
    groundnut oil for deep-frying

For the batter
125g plain flour
Good pinch of sea salt
1 egg yolk
175ml ice-cold sparkling water

To serve
Lemon wedges

Firstly, separate the flowers from each courgette and check your flowers for insects (especially if you have vegetarians coming for supper). Set the flowers aside.

Slice the courgettes as thinly as you can. In a large frying pan, warm a slug of olive oil over a medium-low heat, then add the courgette slices with the garlic. Season with a sprinkling of salt to help draw out moisture and cook slowly for about 10 minutes until they are concentrated and oily, but not at all watery, stirring from time to time; don't let them brown more than a shade. Let cool slightly.

Carefully spoon the cooked courgette mixture into the courgette flowers. You should get 2–4 heaped teaspoonfuls into each one, depending on the size of the flowers.

Heat a 10cm depth of oil in a suitable deep, heavy-based saucepan until it registers 180°C on a frying thermometer, or until a cube of white bread dropped into the oil turns golden brown in just under a minute.

In the meantime, make the batter: sift the flour and salt together into a large mixing bowl, then whisk in the egg yolk and sparkling water.

Cook 2–4 courgette flowers at a time, depending on their size and the diameter of your pan: dip the stuffed flowers into the batter to coat, then carefully lower them into the hot oil. Deep-fry for 1–2 minutes, until puffed up, crisp and golden brown. Drain on kitchen paper. Sprinkle with flaky salt and serve at once, with lemon wedges for squeezing.

Baby courgette salad
with lemon and sugar snap peas

This is as refreshing as it gets. It just cuts through, like the first mouthful of the perfect gin and tonic. Don't be tempted to hold back on the lemons – you'll be pleasantly surprised. It makes a great, zingy starter for a summer lunch, or a lovely side dish alongside some grilled or barbecued lamb chops.

Serves 4 as a starter, 6 as a side dish

4–6 baby courgettes
130g young, tender sugar snap peas
2 organic (unwaxed) lemons
Small bunch of mint, tough stems removed, finely chopped
Small bunch of dill, large stems removed, finely chopped
2 tbsp olive oil
Sea salt and freshly ground black pepper
Borage flowers, to garnish (optional)

Slice the courgettes into rounds, 3mm thick. Throw them into a bowl with the sugar snap peas. Peel one of the lemons, removing all the white pith, then cut out the segments, free from their membranes. Add to the courgettes.

Grate over the zest of the other lemon, being careful to avoid any of the bitter white pith. Halve the lemon and squeeze over the juice. Add the chopped herbs, along with the olive oil, salt and pepper, and toss well.

Leave the salad to stand for 5–10 minutes before serving, to allow the flavours to mingle. Toss again lightly before serving and check the seasoning. Scatter some borage flowers over the salad to garnish if available.

Jerusalem artichoke salad
with goat's cheese and hazelnuts

This is a lovely way to enjoy Jerusalem artichokes. Don't expect them to roast like potatoes – you should get crisp and golden skins, but the insides will be fluffy and may break up a bit. If they do, it just means they will absorb more of the flavours of the hazelnut oil and lemon juice, which is exactly what you want.

Serves 4–6 as a starter or light lunch

80g shelled hazelnuts
650g Jerusalem artichokes
4 tbsp extra-virgin olive oil
Maldon sea salt
1–2 bay leaves
1 tsp hazelnut oil
½ lemon

Freshly ground black pepper
80g firm goat's cheese, cut into
  small chunks
2 handfuls or so of winter salad leaves,
  such as mizuna, rocket and green
  salad bowl lettuce (many of the
  oriental leaves also work well)

First, toast the hazelnuts. Preheat the oven to 180°C/Gas Mark 4. Spread the nuts out in a single layer on a baking sheet and roast for 8–10 minutes, until lightly coloured and the skins are blistered and cracked. Tip them on to a clean tea towel and wrap them up. Leave for a minute, then rub vigorously in the tea towel until the skins fall off. Set aside to cool, then chop the nuts roughly (or leave them whole, if you prefer).

Turn up the oven to 190°C/Gas Mark 5 and put a large roasting tin inside to heat up. Scrub the artichokes thoroughly and halve or quarter them lengthways, depending on their size (you want chunks about 1.5cm thick). Put the artichokes into a bowl and add 3 tbsp of the olive oil, along with 1 tsp salt and the bay leaf. Toss to mix, then tip into the hot roasting tin and roast until lightly golden, about 35 minutes, giving the tray a good shake after 15 minutes to turn the artichokes over in the oil. Set aside to cool slightly.

Meanwhile, whisk together the remaining 1 tbsp olive oil and the hazelnut oil. Drizzle over the warm artichokes, squeeze on a good spritz of lemon juice and season with salt and a few grinds of black pepper. Turn it all over gently with your hands until well combined, then add the hazelnuts, goat's cheese and salad leaves. Toss lightly, divide between plates and serve.

Baby pea and ricotta salad
with spring onions

This salad is a great summer favourite at River Cottage HQ. The sweetness of the peas combined with the creaminess of the ricotta and sharpness of the spring onions is a real winner.

Serves 4 as a starter or light lunch

500g very fresh baby peas
3 tbsp olive oil
10–12 spring onions, trimmed and
  halved lengthways
1 tbsp lemon juice

Sea salt and freshly ground black
  pepper
200g ricotta (or other soft, fresh
  curdy cheese)
1 tsp thyme leaves, roughly chopped

Bring a saucepan of water to the boil, drop in the peas and cook for a maximum of 2 minutes, then drain well.

Heat 1 tbsp olive oil in a frying pan, add the spring onions and sweat gently for 4–5 minutes, until softened.

For the dressing, in a large bowl, combine the rest of the olive oil with the lemon juice and plenty of salt and pepper.

Toss the warm peas and spring onions in the dressing, then divide between individual serving bowls. Crumble the ricotta and scatter over the salad, along with the thyme. Serve warm or at room temperature.

Feta and beetroot salad
with parsley

This makes a gorgeous salad – I promise it tastes just as good as it looks.

Serves 4 as a starter or lunch

500g whole baby beetroot
1 garlic clove, peeled and roughly
    chopped
Sea salt and freshly ground black
    pepper
2 tbsp olive oil
200g feta, or semi-hard goat's cheese,
    such as Woolsery, crumbled into
    small chunks
20g flat-leaf parsley leaves

For the vinaigrette
3 tbsp olive oil
1 tbsp wine, sherry or cider vinegar
Pinch of sugar

To serve
Slices of brown bread

Preheat the oven to 200°C/Gas Mark 6. Scrub the beetroot well and place them on a large piece of foil. Scatter with the garlic, salt and pepper, and trickle over the olive oil. Scrunch up the foil to make a loose parcel and place on a baking tray. Roast until tender – about an hour, although they make take longer. Test with a knife: the beetroot are ready when the blade slips in easily.

Leave the beetroot to cool, then top and tail them and remove their skins. Cut into chunks (quarters or eighths) and place in a large bowl. Add the cheese and parsley leaves and toss the lot together with your hands.

In a small bowl, whisk together the ingredients for the vinaigrette, seasoning with salt and pepper to taste. Drizzle over the salad and toss lightly. Serve straight away, with some brown bread on the side.

Roasted beetroot pizza
with kale and anchovies

Beetroot is so underrated. Its rich, earthy flavour, silky smooth texture and wonderful sweetness make it able to star in both sweet and savoury courses. The combination of beetroot, kale and anchovies makes for a stunning warm salad with some sliced boiled eggs or a bit of sirloin steak, but it also makes a rather spectacular winter pizza topping, with the fragrant oil drizzled over the top.

Roast the beetroot with the skin on, and the roots and leaves intact, to keep in all the flavour. Garlic and thyme are a must – the combination infuses both beetroot and olive oil with the most delicious savour.

Serves 4

For the pizza bases
250g strong plain white bread flour
250g plain flour
2 tsp salt
5g fast-acting dried yeast
350ml warm water
Slug of olive oil

For the topping
5–6 smallish beetroot, with leaves
   and roots intact
4 tbsp olive oil

5 garlic cloves, unpeeled and
   bashed a bit
5–6 thyme sprigs, plus about
   ½ tsp thyme leaves for
   sprinkling on the pizzas
2–3 rosemary sprigs
Sea salt and freshly ground black
   pepper
100g young kale, stalks removed
2 dried chillies, deseeded and chopped
About 300g good mozzarella, torn
24 anchovies or salted pilchards

First make the pizza dough. Sift the flours and salt into a large mixing bowl, stir in the yeast, then make a well in the centre and add most of the water. Using two fingers of one hand, mix until you have a very rough, soft dough, adding more water if the dough is dry. Add the olive oil and squidge it all together.

Turn the dough out on to a well-floured surface and knead until smooth and silky (or you could use an electric mixer with a dough hook attachment). Place the dough in a bowl, cover with a damp tea towel and leave to rise in a warm place until doubled in size, which should take about an hour or so.

Meanwhile, roast the beetroot. Preheat the oven to 200°C/Gas Mark 6. Put your beetroot into a roasting tin with 2–3 tbsp of the olive oil, 3 garlic cloves and the thyme and rosemary sprigs. Roll the beetroot around a bit so that they are nicely coated and season well with salt and pepper. Roast for about 40 minutes, shaking the tin from time to time, until the beetroot are very soft when pierced with a knife. Leave until cool enough to handle, then rub off the skins, chop off the roots and leaves, and slice the beets into wedges. Reserve any of the tasty oil for later.

Turn your oven up as high as it will go and place a couple of sturdy large baking sheets inside to heat up.

Chop the kale roughly. Peel and slice the remaining 2 garlic cloves. Warm 1–2 tbsp olive oil in a frying pan over a high heat and toss in the kale, along with the garlic and chillies. Keep moving the kale around the pan until it's wilted, very soft and any liquid has evaporated. Season with salt and pepper to taste.

When the pizza dough has doubled in size, turn it out on to a lightly floured surface and divide into four. Shape one of the quarters into a circle and then roll it out with a rolling pin until you have a pleasingly thin base. Repeat with the rest of the dough.

Carefully place the pizza bases on the hot baking sheets, then quickly divide the roasted beetroot among them, along with some torn mozzarella and anchovies. Season with salt and pepper, and sprinkle lightly with thyme leaves, then spoon over any leftover beetroot roasting juices.

Bake the pizzas for about 8–10 minutes until the cheese has melted and the base is crisp and browned.

Variations

The pizza dough can be used as the base for so many mouthwatering toppings – you'll probably already have your own favourites. Almost any veg will work if you find its best partners.

Spring into summer tart

If you ever wondered what 'green' would taste like – try this tart. It's bursting with all kinds of fresh and delightful flavours and is exactly what I'd like to eat on a warm summer's day, with a simply dressed salad of baby leaves on the side. More green, I know, but you can't have too much of a good thing.

Serves 6

For the pastry
125g plain flour
Good pinch of salt
75g unsalted butter, chilled and cut
    into small cubes
1 egg, separated
3–4 tbsp cold milk

For the filling
100g fresh garden peas
100g baby broad beans
Knob of butter
1 large bunch of spring onions,
    finely sliced
100g broad bean and pea tops

Small handful of chard leaves, washed
Sea salt and freshly ground black
    pepper
A few feathery fennel tops, chopped
Small bunch of young, flat-leaf
    parsley, stalks removed, leaves
    roughly chopped
Small bunch of mint, stalks removed,
    leaves roughly chopped
Small bunch of chives, finely chopped
75g hard goat's or sheep's cheese,
    coarsely grated
100ml whole milk
200ml double cream
2 whole eggs, plus 2 egg yolks

To make the pastry, put the flour, salt and butter into a food processor and pulse until the mixture is the consistency of coarse breadcrumbs. Add the egg yolk, then with the motor running, pour in the milk, in a thin stream through the funnel. Watch carefully and stop adding the milk as soon as the dough comes together. Tip the pastry on to a lightly floured surface, gently shape into a smooth ball and then flatten slightly to a circle. Wrap in cling film and chill in the fridge for 30 minutes.

Preheat the oven to 170°C/Gas Mark 3. In the meantime, for the filling, blanch the peas and broad beans in a pan of boiling water for 1 minute then refresh in ice water. Drain and set aside. Heat the butter in a frying pan over a medium heat and gently fry the spring onions for 2–3 minutes until soft. Add the broad bean and pea tops, and the chard, and cook for just a couple of minutes until wilted. Season well.

Lightly grease a loose-bottomed 25cm tart tin. Roll out the pastry thinly and line the tin with it, leaving the excess pastry hanging over the edge. Prick the base all over with a fork, line the case with baking paper and baking beans and put the tin on a baking sheet. Bake 'blind' for about 15 minutes. Remove the paper and beans and bake for another 10 minutes.

Lightly beat the egg white, brush some of it over the hot pastry and return the pastry case to the oven for a further 5 minutes; this helps to seal the pastry and prevent any filling leaking out. Trim off the excess pastry using a small, sharp knife or by rolling a rolling pin over the top of the tin so that all of the overhanging pastry falls away.

Turn up the oven to 180°C/Gas Mark 4. Arrange the chard, spring onion and pea top mixture over the bottom of the pastry case. Scatter over the blanched peas and broad beans and then the chopped herbs. Sprinkle on the grated cheese. In a jug, whisk together the milk, cream, eggs and egg yolks, season well with salt and pepper, and pour into the tart case. Bake for about 40 minutes or until lightly set and golden brown. Serve warm or cold.

Variations
Any green spring or summer veg – including asparagus – will work, and the leafy herbs can be altered to suit your taste.

Mackerel with sorrel sauce

This takes only a couple of minutes to throw together and makes a great quick supper. The sharp, lemony tang of sorrel is the perfect foil for the rich, oily flesh of the mackerel.

Serves 2

200g sorrel
4 very fresh mackerel fillets
Sea salt and freshly ground black
    pepper
1 tsp olive oil
50g unsalted butter

1 egg yolk
1 tbsp double cream

To serve
New potatoes

Wash the sorrel thoroughly, remove and discard the stalks and chop the leaves coarsely. Set aside.

Season the mackerel fillets with a little salt and pepper. Put a heavy-based frying pan over a medium heat and add a thin film of olive oil. When the oil is fairly hot, lay the mackerel fillets skin side down in the pan and cook until the flesh is almost completely white. Flip the fillets over for just a minute to finish cooking – the whole process should take no more than 5 minutes. Transfer to a warm plate and keep warm while you make the sauce.

Add the butter to the pan in which you cooked the fish and melt over a medium heat. When it is foaming, throw in the sorrel, which will quickly wilt and turn a dull greeny-brown. Give it a swift stir, remove the pan from the heat and let it cool for 30 seconds, then beat in the egg yolk to thicken the sauce. Season with salt and pepper to taste, and stir in the cream to enrich the sauce.

Serve the mackerel with the warm sorrel sauce and some waxy new potatoes.

Turnip 'risotto'

Turnips are often seen as rather modest fare, which is a great shame as I really love their peppery flavour. If you need convincing – or are just after a top supper – try this recipe by Italian-American chef Mario Batali from his book *Simple Italian Food*. It turns the humble turnip into the star, giving it the full-on glamour treatment. It's lovely as it is, but sometimes I add a little fried pancetta or bacon just for a change.

Serves 4 as a main course, 6 as a starter

500ml hot chicken stock
90ml extra-virgin olive oil
1 medium red onion, peeled and
  finely diced
700g turnips, peeled and cut into
  4–5mm dice

Sea salt and freshly ground black
  pepper
30g unsalted butter
20g Parmesan, freshly grated
Small handful of parsley, tough stalks
  removed, leaves finely chopped

Heat the chicken stock in a pan to a simmer and keep hot. Warm the olive oil in a large, heavy-based frying pan over a medium-low heat. Toss in the onion and cook until softened, about 10 minutes. Add the turnips and cook for 2 minutes.

Ladle in some of the hot chicken stock and cook until absorbed, stirring from time to time. Continue until all of the stock has been added, about 10–15 minutes.

Season with salt and pepper to taste. Stir in the butter and Parmesan, then remove from the heat, scatter over the chopped parsley, and serve in warm bowls.

Squash risotto
with crispy sage

If the taste of tomato encapsulates summer, then squash is surely the same for autumn. It shares a perfect partnership with sage's meaty, aromatic warmth – used here as an undercurrent of flavour and a crispy topping. As the evenings cool and darken, you'll be hard-pressed to find a more comforting supper.

Serves 4 as a main course

900ml vegetable stock (see p.259) or chicken stock
1 medium onion, chopped
3 tbsp olive oil
12 sage leaves, finely chopped, about 2 tbsp
1–2 garlic cloves, chopped
250g arborio rice
Small glass of white wine

375g squash or pumpkin (peeled weight), diced small

To finish
3 tbsp sunflower oil
About 16 sage leaves
75g butter
Piece of Parmesan or Pecorino
Sea salt and freshly ground pepper

Heat the stock in a pan until almost boiling, and then keep hot over a very low heat. In a heavy-based saucepan, sweat the onion in the olive oil until soft but not browned, about 10–15 minutes. Add the chopped sage and garlic and cook for a couple of minutes. Now add the rice and stir to coat the grains with the oil, then add the wine and stir until most of the liquid has been absorbed.

Pour in about a third of the hot stock and bring to a gentle simmer. Cook until almost all the stock has been absorbed, stirring regularly but not all the time. Add the squash and a little more stock, and continue to simmer gently, stirring occasionally, until the stock has been absorbed. Continue to add more stock a little at a time until the pumpkin is soft and the rice is nicely al dente. You may not need all of the stock. The texture of the finished risotto should be loose and creamy.

When it is almost ready, heat the sunflower oil in a small pan and fry the whole sage leaves for a few seconds until crisp. Drain on kitchen paper.

Now it's time for the final stage that adds so much of the creaminess to the dish. Stir the butter and a little grated cheese into the risotto and season well. Divide between warm serving bowls and throw a few crispy sage leaves over each portion. Bring the rest of the cheese and a grater to the table for guests to help themselves.

Variations

Courgettes, asparagus, broad beans, peas, lettuce, spinach and many others will happily take the place of the squash in this recipe. And rosemary (used lightly) works well in place of the sage.

Celeriac rémoulade

Rémoulade is, strictly speaking, a mustardy French dressing that could be used with whatever you fancy, but such is its happy friendship with celeriac, I've never known it served in any other way. This is the dish to give anyone who might need convincing about the wonder of celeriac.

Serves 6–8 as a side dish

2 tsp hot English mustard
2 tsp cider vinegar
1 scant tsp sugar
Pinch of sea salt

75ml olive oil
75ml groundnut or sunflower oil
1 celeriac, about 750g

Combine the mustard, cider vinegar, sugar and salt in a bowl. Pour the oils into a jug, then very slowly whisk them into the mustard mixture until you get a creamy, emulsified dressing. Taste and adjust the seasoning with salt if necessary.

Peel the celeriac and cut it into fine matchsticks, then toss them in the dressing to coat evenly.

You can serve this salad with almost anything, but it is especially good with cold pork or ham and sourdough bread.

Variations

Although perfect with celeriac, this dressing works really well with almost anything hot or cold. Try it with some of the brassicas, salad leaves, asparagus, globe artichokes or summer carrots.

French beans
with Japanese-style dressing

I love the contrast between the intensely green beans and dramatic black dressing in this recipe. It's great alongside simply grilled or barbecued fish. Alternatively, you can add some shredded leftover roast chicken or pork to transform it into a main course in its own right. The dressing is good with other vegetables, too, especially carrots and courgettes.

Serves 4 as a side dish

300g French beans
50g black sesame seeds
1 tsp hemp seeds
1 tsp sunflower seeds

2 tbsp caster sugar
1 tbsp soy sauce
½ tbsp mirin
1 tsp toasted sesame oil

Top the beans (tail them, too, if you want, though I rather like the curling tails, so tend to leave them on). Plunge them into a pan of boiling water and cook for a couple of minutes until they're just beginning to soften but haven't lost their bite. Drain, refresh in a bowl of iced water, then drain again and pat dry.

Warm a small frying pan over a medium heat and toss in the sesame seeds, hemp seeds and sunflower seeds. Shake the pan until the seeds are just toasted and releasing their fragrance – this will take only a couple of minutes. Lightly crush the toasted seeds using a pestle and mortar, then add the sugar, soy sauce, mirin and sesame oil, and mix to a paste. It should have the texture of coarse, damp sand.

Use your hands to toss the blanched French beans with the dressing, making sure that they are all well coated, then serve.

Variations
This fantastic dressing works well on anything from broad beans to salad leaves. Try it with whatever you like to dress.

Honey roast carrots

These are a great favourite over the winter months at River Cottage HQ – we make them all the time. They are so easy and quick to throw together, but be warned – their luscious, caramelised sweetness is quite addictive.

Serves 6 as a side dish

2–3 tbsp olive oil or goose fat
1kg good-quality carrots (either from your garden or organic), peeled
1–2 tbsp good runny honey (preferably local)

Sea salt and freshly ground black pepper
40g unsalted butter
Small bunch of flat-leaf parsley, tough stalks removed, leaves roughly chopped

Preheat your oven to 200°C/Gas Mark 6. Put the olive oil or goose fat into a roasting tin and put the tin into the oven to heat up.

Slice the carrots and tip them into the hot roasting tin. Spoon over the honey and season with salt and pepper, then shake the tin a little until the carrots are well coated. Roast for 35–40 minutes, giving the tin a good shake halfway through the cooking time. The carrots are done when they are tender, crisp and darkened around the edges. Stir in the butter and chopped parsley and serve immediately.

Variations

Parsnips and the other root vegetables take to this treatment really well. Jerusalem artichokes work too, but I'd recommend halving the amount of honey.

Dauphinoise potatoes

This meltingly delicious dauphinoise has more of a garlicky kick than the traditional recipe, where the gratin dish is simply rubbed with a single clove, which is then discarded. By all means substitute any other root veg for the potato, or better still, use half potato and half a different root veg.

Serves 6 as a side dish

25g unsalted butter, softened
600g waxy potatoes, such as 'Belle de Fontenay' or 'Duke of York'
300ml double cream

2 large garlic cloves, peeled and crushed or grated
Sea salt and freshly ground black pepper

Preheat the oven to 170°C/Gas Mark 3. Rub a gratin dish liberally with the butter.

Peel the potatoes and slice them thinly, either with a sharp knife or a mandoline. In a large bowl, whisk together the cream and garlic and season well with salt and pepper. Toss the potatoes in the mixture and layer them in the gratin dish, then pour over any remaining cream.

Bake for 1¼–1½ hours, pressing down all over with a fish slice or spatula every 15 minutes or so, to compress the potatoes and stop them from drying out. Alternatively, cover tightly with foil for the first hour of cooking, then remove the foil and turn up the heat to 200°C/Gas Mark 6 for the last 15 minutes. The potato bake is ready when the top is bubbling and golden, and the potatoes are soft and yielding when pierced with a knife. Leave to stand for a few minutes before serving.

Variations

Turnips, celeriac, parsnips and squash all work particularly well in this dauphinoise – but are best as a half-and-half split with the potatoes rather than used exclusively, as their sweetness can be a little too much on its own.

Creamy Brussels sprouts
with chestnuts and bacon

If you know anyone who's yet to be convinced by Brussels sprouts, put them out of their misery and cook this dish for them. It's so undeniably magnificent that it will convert them in a second.

Serves 6 as a side dish, 2 for supper

250g fresh chestnuts (or use vacuum-packed chestnuts)
500g Brussels sprouts
Sea salt

Knob of butter
2 tbsp double cream
4–6 thick streaky bacon rashers

Roast the chestnuts well ahead: make a little cut in each one (to prevent explosions) and dry-fry them in a heavy-based frying pan over a medium-high heat for about 10–15 minutes (or, better still, toast them on a shovel in an open fire). Turn them frequently until they are cooked through and probably a little charred. Let the chestnuts cool, then peel away both the shell and the thin brown inner skin. Chop or crumble them up and they're ready to go.

Just before serving, add the Brussels sprouts to a saucepan of well-salted water and simmer for around 6–8 minutes, depending on their size, until just tender. Drain well, then purée with the butter and double cream in a food processor, or using a hand-held stick blender. You're after creaminess, but the texture doesn't have to be totally smooth.

Cut each bacon rasher into bite-sized pieces and fry them in a dry pan until crispy.

Add the chestnuts to the creamed sprouts and heat through gently but thoroughly. Spoon the mixture into a warmed serving dish and sprinkle over the crispy bacon bits. Serve immediately.

Variations
All of the leafy brassicas will happily partner the chestnuts, cream and bacon.

Glutney

This is one of those marvellous recipes that you'll turn to again and again. Try it once and you'll see how easy it is to play around with the ingredients – stick to the approximate overall amount and you'll find it's very forgiving. This year I made it with squash instead of courgettes, and plums in place of tomatoes, and (if you'll forgive the immodesty) it was outstanding.

Makes about 10 x 340g jars

1kg courgettes, unpeeled if small, peeled if huge, cut into 1cm dice
500g onions, peeled and diced
1kg red or green tomatoes, scalded, skinned and roughly chopped
1kg cooking or eating apples, peeled and diced
500g sultanas or raisins
500g light brown sugar
750ml white wine (or cider) vinegar

1–3 tsp dried chilli flakes
1 tsp salt

For the spice bag
1 thumb-sized nugget of fresh or dried ginger, roughly chopped
12 cloves
12 black peppercorns
1 (generous) tsp coriander seeds
A few blades of mace

Put the vegetables and fresh fruit into a large, heavy-based pan with the sultanas and sugar. Make the wine vinegar up to 1 litre with water and add to the pan with the chilli flakes and salt.

Make up the spice bag by tying all the spices together in a square of muslin. Add the spice bag to the pan, pushing it into the middle.

Heat the mixture gently, stirring occasionally until the sugar has dissolved, then slowly bring to the boil. Simmer, uncovered, for 2–3 hours, stirring regularly to ensure it does not burn on the bottom of the pan. The chutney is ready when it is rich, thick and reduced. To test, drag a wooden spoon through the mixture: it should part to form a channel and reveal the base of the pan. If it starts to dry out before this stage is reached, add a little boiling water. Allow to cool slightly.

Pot the chutney while still warm in sterilised jars. Seal with plastic-coated screw-top lids (essential to stop the vinegar interacting with the metal). Leave to mature for at least 2 weeks – ideally 2 months – before using.

Variations
Vary the summer veg and fruit with whatever takes your fancy.

Salsa verde

The sauce as far as I'm concerned. I've yet to find any meat, fish or poultry it doesn't go with – and the more you make it the better it gets, as you develop a feel for how you like it. The herbs, and their individual quantities, are yours to choose. I favour tarragon and chervil, but tend to avoid rosemary and sage, as they are inclined to dominate the others. Try the recipe below and take it off in your own direction.

Serves 4

1 garlic clove, peeled
Small bunch of flat-leaf parsley,
    leaves stripped from stalks
Small bunch of basil
Slightly smaller bunch of mint,
    leaves stripped from stalks
2 anchovies

2 tsp capers
1 tsp mustard
A few drops of lemon juice
½ tsp sugar
Pinch of sea salt
Freshly ground black pepper
2 tbsp olive oil

Roughly chop the garlic, then add the herbs and chop together until combined. Add the anchovies and capers and continue until everything is finely chopped.

In a bowl, combine the mustard, lemon juice, sugar, salt and pepper, then stir in the herby mix. Stir in the olive oil a little at a time, to obtain a thick, glossy consistency. Now's the time to taste it – and add a little of this or that until it's as you want it.

Pesto

Of course you'll be tempted to use a food processor to make this classic dressing, but try to make it with a pestle and mortar, at least once. The texture is better and it's a satisfying thing to do. Pesto is something you should taste and tweak as you go along, so adjust the quantities until you get the flavour that is right for you.

Serves 4

½ garlic clove, peeled and chopped
Sea salt and freshly ground
   black pepper
3 good handfuls of basil, leaves
   picked from the stalks and
   roughly chopped

Handful of pine nuts, very
   lightly toasted
Good handful of freshly grated
   Parmesan
Extra-virgin olive oil
Squeeze of lemon juice (optional)

Pound the garlic with a little pinch of salt and the basil leaves in a pestle and mortar, or pulse in a food processor but be careful not to over-process. Add the pine nuts and pound again. Turn into a bowl and add half the Parmesan. Stir gently and add just enough olive oil to bind the sauce and get to an oozy consistency. Season to taste, then add most of the remaining cheese. Pour in some more oil and taste again. Keep adding a bit more cheese or oil until you're happy with the taste and consistency. You may like to add a squeeze of lemon juice at the end to give it a little tang, but it's not essential. Try it with and without and see which you prefer.

Hollandaise sauce

Hugh's cheaty hollandaise is *the* match for all the headline veg that one by one herald in the warmer months – purple sprouting broccoli, asparagus, peas, etc.

Serves 4

150g unsalted butter
1 egg yolk

Good squeeze of lemon juice
Sea salt and freshly ground pepper

Melt the butter gently, cool slightly, then whisk it, a little at a time, into the egg yolk, aiming for a loose mayonnaise consistency. Whisk in the lemon juice and season with salt and pepper. Serve soon after making, as this sauce has a tendency to split after a while. Even if it does start to split, fortunately it's still quite palatable.

Roasted tomato sauce

As simple and delicious as it gets, this is perfect as a quick midweek sauce for pasta, a pizza topping, the base of any number of soups and much, much more. Any flavoursome tomato variety will work well, but in truth, this sauce even brings out redeeming qualities in a fairly ordinary harvest. And you can always throw oregano, thyme and/or a little chilli into the mix before roasting if you fancy.

Serves 4–6, or more

1kg ripe tomatoes ('San Marzano' are perfect)
3 garlic cloves, peeled and chopped

3 tbsp olive oil
Sea salt and freshly ground black pepper

Preheat the oven to 180°C/Gas Mark 4. Halve the tomatoes and lay them cut side up in an ovenproof dish. Mix the garlic with the olive oil and spoon it over the tomatoes. Season with salt and pepper. Roast for 40 minutes or so, until the tomatoes soften and begin to char slightly. Push the garlicky, tomatoey mix through a sieve to remove the skins and seeds. Taste the sauce and adjust the seasoning if you need to. That, believe it or not, is it.

Vegetable stock

This recipe from the River Cottage kitchen makes a lovely, fresh, well-flavoured stock that you can use as the base for any number of soups, risottos, stews and more. The quantities listed show you the proportions – simply multiply up if you're in the mood to make plenty to freeze.

Makes about 1.5 litres

3 large onions
6 carrots
1 head of celery
Handful of parsley sprigs
Handful of thyme sprigs

4 bay leaves

Optionals
Fennel
Parsley stalks

Finely shred everything you're using, place in a large pan and just cover with water. Bring to the boil, simmer for 2 minutes, then take off the heat. Leave to infuse for 30 minutes, then strain. Freeze any stock you're not using in half-litre batches.

Carrot and walnut cake

Fragrant with spices and deliciously moist, this cake is about as far away from the dry and dreary 1970s health-food shop incarnations as you can get. The unusual addition of apple sauce keeps it really juicy. You can either make your own apple sauce by cooking one large Bramley apple in a couple of tablespoons of water until fluffy, or use good-quality ready-made.

Makes 12 squares

80g sultanas
Knob of butter, for greasing
220g wholemeal self-raising flour
1 tsp baking powder
1 tsp ground cinnamon
1 tsp ground ginger
½ tsp salt
Good pinch of ground cloves
220g light muscovado sugar, plus
   an extra 3 tbsp for the syrup

120ml sunflower oil
Finely grated zest and juice of
   1 orange
2 eggs, lightly beaten
225g apple sauce (see above)
270g carrots, peeled and coarsely
   grated
80g walnuts, roughly chopped
1 tbsp lemon juice

Preheat the oven to 170°C/Gas Mark 3. Put the sultanas into a small bowl, pour on hot water to cover and leave to soak for 20 minutes.

Lightly grease a loose-bottomed 20–22cm square cake tin, about 8cm deep, line the base with greaseproof paper and butter the paper. Sift together the flour, baking powder, cinnamon, ginger, salt and ground cloves.

In a large bowl, whisk together the 220g muscovado sugar, oil and orange zest until well combined, then whisk in the eggs until the mixture is creamy. Fold in the apple sauce, followed by the flour mixture until just combined. Next fold in the grated carrots and walnuts. Finally, drain the sultanas and fold these in.

Spoon the mixture into the prepared tin and smooth the surface with a spatula. Bake for about 1¼ hours, until a fine skewer inserted into the centre comes out without crumbs clinging to it. If the cake appears to be overbrowning before it is done, cover the top loosely with foil.

While the cake is in the oven, make the syrup. Put the orange juice into a small saucepan with the 3 tbsp light muscovado sugar and 1 tbsp lemon juice. Warm over a low heat, stirring until the sugar dissolves, then increase the heat and simmer until slightly syrupy, about 4–5 minutes.

As you remove the cake from the oven, run a knife around the edge and pierce the top a few times with a fine skewer. Now pour over the syrup, trying to make sure that you cover the surface fairly evenly. Stand the cake tin on a wire rack and leave to cool for a while before cutting into squares. You can serve this cake warm as a pudding with a dollop of crème fraîche, or cold as a treat at any time.

Variations
For a different sweet alternative to the carrot, try using parsnip or beetroot.

Pumpkin meringue pie

This ginger-spiked pastry case with its silky, spicy pumpkin filling and wispy topping of crisp-on-the-outside, soft-on-the-inside meringue makes a pretty spectacular autumn dessert. You'll hardly believe anything quite so glamorous started life in the veg patch.

Serves 10

For the filling
1.4kg pumpkin(s)
30g unsalted butter
50g light muscovado sugar, plus an extra 20g for sprinkling
1 tbsp syrup from the stem ginger jar
1 tsp ground ginger
1 tsp ground cinnamon
Good pinch of ground nutmeg
Good pinch of cloves
Pinch of salt
3 egg yolks
100ml double cream

For the pastry
450g plain flour
140g unrefined icing sugar

Pinch of salt
½ tsp ground ginger
30g preserved stem ginger in syrup, drained and finely chopped
225g unsalted butter, well chilled and cubed
2 egg yolks
3–4 tbsp iced water

For the meringue
3 egg whites
175g golden caster sugar

To serve (optional)
Whipped cream, a little extra chopped stem ginger and a drizzle of syrup from the jar

Preheat the oven to 180°C/Gas Mark 4. Halve the pumpkin(s) and scoop out the seeds. Put a small knob of butter and sprinkle 1 tsp light muscovado sugar into each cavity. Place in a roasting tin, cavities facing up. Put a splash of water into the bottom of the tin, cover tightly with foil and bake until the pumpkin is completely tender, about 1 hour.

Meanwhile, make the pastry. Sift together the flour, icing sugar, salt and ground ginger. Tip into a food processor and add the stem ginger and cubes of butter. Pulse until the mixture resembles coarse sand, then add the egg yolks and pulse quickly until it comes together in a ball, adding a little iced water if you need to, 1 tbsp at a time. Wrap the dough in cling film and chill in the fridge for about 30 minutes.

Let the pumpkin cool slightly, then scoop out the flesh and buttery juices into a food processor (you should have about 500g). Add the muscovado sugar, ginger syrup, spices and salt, and purée until very smooth. In a separate bowl, whisk the egg yolks and cream together, then fold in the pumpkin mixture until well combined.

Lightly grease a loose-bottomed 30cm flan tin, 3cm deep. Unwrap the pastry and roll out between two sheets of lightly floured baking parchment (this makes it slightly easier to handle) to a large round. Gently lower the pastry into the flan tin, easing it into the edges and being careful not to stretch it. Allow the excess pastry to hang over the side of the tin and stand the tin on a baking sheet.

Line the pastry case with baking paper and baking beans and bake 'blind' for 20 minutes. Remove the paper and beans, prick the tart base with a fork and return to the oven for 10 minutes. Leave to cool completely. Use a sharp knife to remove the excess pastry from the edge, or roll a rolling pin over the top and let the excess fall away. Heat the oven to 150°C/Gas Mark 2.

For the meringue, whisk the egg whites in a large clean bowl until they form stiff peaks. Whisk in the sugar, 1 tbsp at a time, until the mixture is thick and glossy.

Spoon the pumpkin filling into the pastry case, smooth with a spatula, then spread the meringue over the top with a palette knife, making sure it seals the edges completely. Swirl decoratively with your knife. Bake for 45 minutes.

Serve the pumpkin meringue pie warm or cold, with whipped cream, a scattering of chopped stem ginger and a drizzle of ginger syrup if you like.

Directory

Seeds and seedlings

The Heritage Seed Library
www.gardenorganic.org.uk/hsl
024 7630 8210
Members receive free heirloom
varieties, which helps to conserve our
edible heritage

The Real Seed Catalogue
www.realseeds.co.uk
01239 821107
Excellent small supplier – no F1 or
GM seeds

Kings Seeds
www.kingsseeds.com
01376 570000

Edwin Tuckers
www.tuckers-seeds.co.uk
01364 652233

Thomas Etty
www.thomasetty.co.uk
01460 57934

Jekka's Herb Farm
www.jekkasherbfarm.com
0845 290 3255

Nickys Nursery
www.nickys-nursery.co.uk
01843 600972

Sarah Raven's Kitchen and Garden
www.sarahraven.com
0845 092 0283

Rocket Gardens
www.rocketgardens.co.uk
01209 831468
Suppliers of organic vegetable and herb
seedlings to create instant gardens

Delfland Nurseries
www.organicplants.co.uk
01354 740553
A nursery specialising in organic
vegetable seedlings

The Chilli Pepper Company
www.chileseeds.co.uk
01539 558110

South Devon Chilli Farm
www.southdevonchillifarm.co.uk
01548 550782

Other supplies

Fertile fibre
www.fertilefibre.com
01432 853111
Organically certified peat-free compost
and more

West Riding Organics
www.wrorganics.co.uk
01484 609171
Organically certified compost

The Natural Gardener
www.thenaturalgardener.co.uk
01568 611729
Coir and biodegradable pots, compost
and sustainable pest control

LBS Garden Warehouse
www.lbsgardenwarehouse.co.uk
01282 873370
General garden supplies, including
mulch mat/ground cover

The Little Veg Patch
www.earthwormlandscapes.co.uk
01202 882993
Instant raised veg patch

Link-a-bord
www.linkabord.co.uk
01773 590566
Instant raised beds made from recycled
plastic

Wiggly wigglers
www.wigglywigglers.co.uk
01981 500391
Worms, wormeries and general veg
patch supplies

Implementations
www.implementations.co.uk
0845 330 3148
Bronze/copper tools – hardwearing and
beautiful

The Green Gardener
www.greengardener.co.uk
01603 715096
Range of biological pest control, plus
general veg patch supplies

Defenders
www.defenders.co.uk
01233 813121
Biological pest control for the garden

Useful organisations

The River Cottage Community
http://community.rivercottage.net
A community of thousands to call
on for advice and to share experiences

Garden Organic
www.gardenorganic.org.uk
024 7630 3517
A charity (formerly the HDRA)
dedicated to organic growing. Well
worth joining to give you access to a
wealth of advice. Also an excellent
source for seeds and everything to do
with growing

Royal Horticultural Society
www.rhs.org.uk
0845 062 1111
A great source of advice, with
numerous excellent gardens to visit,
and also offers a soil analysis service

Slow Food
www.slowfooduk.info
01584 879599
Promoting the locality, diversity and
enjoyment of food

National Society of Allotment Holders
and Leisure Gardeners
www.nsalg.org.uk
01536 266576
Protecting, preserving and promoting
allotment gardening

My own website is:
www.otterfarm.co.uk

Acknowledgements

Before I had the fun of writing one of my own, I'd never have suspected what a team effort turning the words into a book really is. So this is the part where I come clean about not having done absolutely everything on my own.

If you've tried any of the recipes in this book, you may be convinced that I'm a better cook than I am. Hopefully some of you won't get to read this as it's tucked away at the back and will carry on in blissful ignorance. In truth, without the River Cottage kitchen team as a whole, and Gill Mellor and Debora Robertson in particular, this book's final step on the journey from plot to plate would have been a far less tasty one. Thank you. And to Hugh for letting me pinch the odd classic of his.

Huge thanks also to Gavin Kingcome for his fine photography. And to Cristian Barnett for photographic inspiration, encouragement and advice in equal measure.

I owe much gratitude to Richard Atkinson, Janet Illsley, and Natalie Hunt in particular, at Bloomsbury, for their patience, vision and tireless enthusiasm. And to Will Webb, an inspired designer with a fantastic eye. Together they have done much to make this book what it is.

Thanks also to my agent, the rather wonderful Caroline Michel at PFD, whose enthusiasm and faith in me I hope to repay with endless sales and the second bottle of my own sparkling wine.

To my family, the first bottle. Candida and my lovely daughter Nell, thank you for being entirely unselfish in giving me the time and freedom to write this. As I tend to take half an hour over five minutes, I have much to repay.

Lastly, to those at River Cottage. To Emma Stapleforth, Victoria Moorey and Will Livingstone – they do most of the work and I get too much of the credit – thank you. To Simon Hansford (the previous Head Gardener) and Nikki Duffy: thanks for your contributions early on. To Steven Lamb, who I work so closely with: it's a total pleasure. To Rob Love: I hope this will help you stop fishing (for veg) so much. And Hugh: without whom there would be no book... thanks for thinking I could do it. And to everyone else at RCHQ: going to work couldn't feel less like going to work.

Further reading

I recommend: *Bob Flowerdew's Complete Book of Companion Gardening*; *Salad Leaves for All Seasons: Organic Growing from Pot to Plot* by Charles Dowding; *Oriental Vegetables* by Joy Larkcom; *Jekka's Complete Herb Book* by Jekka McVicar; and *The Allotment Keeper's Handbook: A Down-to-Earth Guide to Growing Your Own Food* by Jane Perrone. And if you're looking for more ideas for what to do with your harvest, these three classics are indispensable – *Jane Grigson's Vegetable Book*, *Sarah Raven's Garden Cookbook* and *The River Cottage Year*.

Index

River Cottage Handbooks

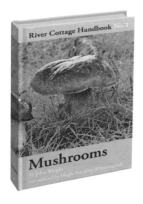

Seasonal, Local, Organic, Wild

FOR FURTHER INFORMATION,
AND TO ORDER ONLINE, VISIT
RIVERCOTTAGE.NET